# A VISION SO NOBLE

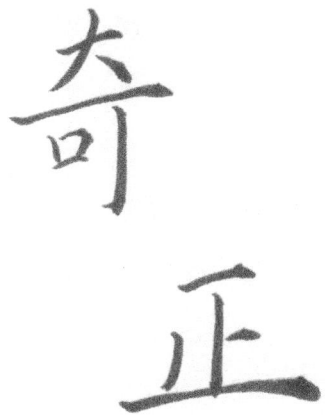

Qi *and* Zheng *represent the unorthodox and the orthodox—
the unexpected and the expected—the unusual and the usual.
Sun-tzu and John Boyd alike favored Qi.*

# A VISION SO NOBLE

*John Boyd,
the OODA Loop, and
America's War on Terror*

Daniel Ford

Warbird Books 2010
Durham, New Hampshire, USA

*". . . a vision rooted in human nature so noble, so attractive that it not only attracts the uncommitted and magnifies the spirit and strength of its adherents, but also undermines the dedication and determination of any competitors or adversaries . . ."*

A VISION SO NOBLE. Copyright © 2010 by Daniel Ford. All rights reserved. Manufactured in the United States of America. No part of this book may be used or reproduced in any manner whatever without written permission, except in the case of brief quotations embodied in critical articles and reviews. For further information, contact Daniel Ford, 433 Bay Road, Durham NH 03824, USA.

Frontispiece calligraphy by Difei Zhang. Except where otherwise indicated in the captions, all other graphics are from the Papers of Colonel John R. Boyd (USAF), U.S. Marine Corps Archives and Special Collections, Quantico, Virginia.

In different form, portions of this text were earlier submitted in partial fulfilment of the requirements for the Master of Arts in War Studies at King's College London.

Published by Warbird Books, April 2010.

ISBN 9781451589818

*John Boyd, well groomed for a change*

# Preface

John Boyd was arguably the most important American military thinker since the late-19th-Century sea power theorist, Admiral Alfred Thayer Mahan. Best known for his formulation of the "OODA Loop" as a model for competitive decision making, Colonel Boyd left his mark as well on air combat tactics, maneuver warfare, and what we now call "fourth-generation warfare." On no branch of the service was his influence greater than on the U.S. Marine Corps. "From John Boyd," wrote General Charles Krulak, then the Marine commander, "we learned about competitive decision making on the battlefield—compressing time, using time as an ally."[1]

An aggressive man, Boyd naturally favored the offense, as exemplified by the *blitzkrieg* or "lightning war" advocated by the

---
[1] Quoted in Hammond 2001, p. 3.

Chinese master Sun-tzu, the German tank commander Heinz Guderian, and the British partisan leader T. E. Lawrence, better known as Lawrence of Arabia. Boyd was less interested in defensive tactics, though in his culminating, fifteen-hour brief, *A Discourse on Winning and Losing*, he did dwell at some length on the problem of what he called "counter-guerrilla" operations.

Boyd died in 1997, after Osama bin Laden's "declaration of war" against the United States, but before America's trauma of September 11, 2001, in which the al-Qaeda leader set us on a course to our subsequent difficulties in Afghanistan and Iraq.[2] Given another ten years of life, Boyd certainly would have addressed the question I attempt to answer here: *How to fight the War on Terror?* How should we have orchestrated our response to the al-Qaeda attacks—or, in the parlance of the 21st Century: how would John Boyd have us fight a fourth-generation war?

I was a college student during the Korean War, and I was drafted soon after graduating, to serve the then-customary two years in an Army essentially the same as the one that landed at Normandy in June 1944. Nor had it changed that much when I bought a ticket to Saigon in 1964, to work for a time as a correspondent for a progressive journal called *The Nation*. In my travels around South Vietnam, I found that Special Forces had acquired a new respectability, along with the iconic green beret and a lightweight rifle that would eventually be adopted as the M-16. Similarly, helicopter pilots had been supplied with Kevlar flak vests (which they usually chose to sit on rather than wear). Such minor improvements apart, the U.S. Army that struggled in the rain forests and paddy fields of Vietnam was identical to the one I'd served somewhat reluctantly a few years before, and that in

---

[2] Bin Laden 1996. I don't mean to suggest that the al-Qaeda leader personally directed these events. As Marc Sageman writes: "When a terrorist network embarks on a major new operation, the people involved do not know exactly how they are going to do it.... Each mujaheed starts with a general notion of what is required of him and improvises with other mujaheed as he goes along" (Sageman 2004, p. 165) ... or does the improvising on his own, as Major Nidal Hasan seems to have done at Fort Hood in October 2009. John Boyd would have felt right at home with this concept.

turn had helped win the Second World War. That was the conception of military operations that I carried into the 21st Century.

But in April 2003, as I followed the invasion of Iraq on real-time television—itself an astonishing innovation—I discovered that my knowledge was badly outdated. American weapons were subtly different; and American troops could see in the dark—indeed, preferred to move at night, whereas in earlier wars their fathers and grandfathers had been notably afraid of the dark. The troops were so accustomed to moving in armored vehicles that men on foot were known as "dismounts." Most surprising of all, to me anyhow, was the sight of American columns running and gunning up both banks of the Euphrates with no apparent concern for securing their rear or maintaining a supply route. This was, I realized, an entirely new sort of warfare.

Accordingly, I signed up for an online master's program at King's College London, where my tutors would be bright young men and women of that institution's War Studies program, and my classmates a medley of mid-career military officers and civilians. About half of them, I suppose, were majors in the British Army. (Not the least of my findings was that, while Britain has a Royal Navy, it doesn't have a Royal Army. It seems that the ground forces were founded by the regicide Oliver Cromwell.) The others were serving officers in the Royal Air Force and the American, Danish, and Swedish armed forces, along with teachers, entrepreneurs, and civil servants from Singapore to Los Angeles, plus a seventy-something journalist from New Hampshire. War in the Modern World was a three-year program based on online textbooks and discussions, plus more reading than anyone possibly could have accomplished. Instead of sitting for exams, we submitted essays—research papers, in American usage.

My final term was given over to what was grandly termed Strategic Dimensions of Contemporary Warfare. Among the strategists, of course, was Carl von Clausewitz (1780-1831), whose *On War* became the foundation of Western military thought. I enjoyed my introduction to the Prussian master, though I agonized over the linear nature of his concept of war, stepping so neatly (as it seemed to me) from Strategy to Planning to Tactics, without any possibility that tactics might in turn influence strategy. Perhaps that worked for the Napoleonic wars, when the strategist and the field commander were one and the same person, but it hardly seemed appropriate in a day when the commander of the U.S. Marines could write in all seriousness of the "strategic corporal"—that is, the young soldier in charge of a fire team who could, by calling in bombs upon a village, affect the standing of a nation.

In my first essay for the course, I tried to make the process circular by applying the Hegelian dialectic, whereby the final term in each triad (thesis—antithesis—synthesis) begins another, similar, and more elegant round. Alas, it didn't work, or at least not well enough. Tactics do indeed influence Strategy, or should, but only in the sense of refining it, not in creating something new. In the end, I punted the effort into the future, hoping that John Boyd and his OODA Loop might provide a way to break out of the Clausewitzian triad. So it proved—or so I argued in my last essay for War in the Modern World.

This small book melds those two essays with my concluding dissertation on how Boyd's theories might be applied to counter-insurgency.[3] Limited respectively to 1,500, 3,000, and 15,000 words, they didn't provide much latitude for expression, so now I take the opportunity to expand on them. In what follows, I discuss John Boyd's written and oral legacy and his influence upon the U.S. military toward the end of the 20th Century, as demonstrated in our two wars against Iraq. I pay particular attention to the relationship Boyd saw between blitzkrieg and guerrilla operations, and the ways in which each might be countered. As a test of his methodology, I advance (and tentatively discard) the U.S. Marines' Combined Action Platoon of the Vietnam War as a solution that he might have embraced.

---

[3] I have posted these online at www.warbirdforum.com/clause1.htm, www.lulu.com/content/5665676, and www.danford.net/boyd/dissertation.pdf.

# Acknowledgements

John Boyd was a career Air Force officer but, perhaps understandably, his thinking made more of an impression upon the U.S. ground forces—and especially the Marine Corps—than upon his own service. His papers as a result were entrusted to the Gray Research Center at Quantico, Virginia. I am grateful to Martha Robinson and her staff at the Marine Corps University for their assistance with this amazing collection, consisting of every document that Boyd composed, and much of what he read, over a twenty-year period.

I am indebted also to Jan Salas and the inter-library loan staff at the University of New Hampshire Library, for their help in retrieving reference books and journals; to Eitan Shamir of King's College London, for supplying documents from his study of mission command; and to Chester Richards, Grant Hammond, Franklin (Chuck) Spinney, and Lonnie Ratley III, for sharing their insights about Boyd's thinking. Finally, a tip of my virtual hat to David Betz, my always-encouraging tutor at King's College, and to Sally Ford for her sharp eye and sharper second guesses.

*– Daniel Ford, Durham, New Hampshire, April 2010*

# 1 - The Mad Major

John Boyd was born in the hardscrabble town of Erie, Pennsylvania, in 1927. His father died when he was three, at the onset of the Great Depression, and he was brought up by his widowed mother, who worked three jobs to rear him and four siblings, one of whom was stricken by polio and another by schizophrenia. Toward the end of World War II, young Boyd enlisted in the U.S. Army Air Forces but was rejected for flight training because of "low aptitude."[4] Instead, the Army put him to work as a swimming instructor in occupied Japan.

Discharged in 1947, he enrolled as an engineering student at the University of Iowa. It wasn't a success. "Academically," as Grant Hammond tells us in his 2001 biography, *The Mind of War*, "Boyd was competent but inconsistent, undisciplined, and occasionally just not interested."[5] He switched his concentration to economics, partied, swam competitively—and joined the Reserve Officers' Training Corps then ubiquitous on American campuses. In 1951, the second year of the Korean War, Boyd earned his bachelor's degree and a commission in the newly fledged United States Air Force. Again he applied for flight training, and this time he demonstrated a considerable aptitude, throwing his North American T-6 trainer "around the sky in such a fearless manner that it seemed to others as if he had done it a thousand times."[6]

Transitioning to jet fighters, Lieutenant Boyd was just as aggressive. "I had to bend the shit out of that airplane," he once boasted of his mock combat with flight instructors and fellow students.[7] He especially enjoyed the lack of structure in flight training in the 1950s, as he recalled on another occasion: "We didn't have any rules when I went into it. It was fantastic. Of

---

[4] Coram 2002, p. 30. This unsourced biography provides colorful detail about Boyd's life, though Hammond 2001 is a more scholarly account.
[5] Hammond 2001, p. 20.
[6] Coram 2002, p. 40.
[7] Boyd 1977, oral history interview, p. 12.

course we killed a lot of guys. We killed more guys in training than we did in Korea."[8] The Air Force did have rules, of course, but Boyd preferred to make his own.

Oddly, for a man often called America's greatest fighter pilot, Boyd was never credited with an air-to-air victory over an enemy aircraft. He reached Korea in March 1953, four months before the armistice was signed, and not time enough to accumulate the thirty missions that would qualify him as a "shooter," instead of a wingman tasked with guarding his flight leader.

Postwar, Boyd was assigned to the USAF Fighter Weapons School at Nellis Air Force Base, Nevada, first as a student, then an instructor. He was a demanding teacher. "If the guy really wants to learn and has some problem," as he explained his system in later years, "you do not have to give him the 2x4. But if the guy has an obstruction"—i.e., had an overly high opinion of his abilities—"I would cut his balls off in 10 seconds."[9] The castration would take the form of an air-to-air humiliation. Boyd began the dogfight as he usually did, with the student directly behind him—"on his six," as pilots say, the six o'clock position being the most advantageous for the attacker—and in under forty seconds reverse their positions, meanwhile shouting "*Guns, guns, guns!*" to let the student know that in the real world he would have been a dead man. In this manner he earned the nickname of Forty Second Boyd.

Boyd loved the freedom he found in aerial combat. And he too was learning. In the air with his students—or a fellow instructor, or a challenger from another airbase—he made one of those connections for which he would become famous. "I had a degree in economics," as he recalled toward the end of his life. What a fighter pilot did in the clear Nevada air, he realized, was not all that different from what John D. Rockefeller had done with Standard Oil, or E. H. Harriman with the Union Pacific railroad. "This is like 19th Century capitalism in the sky!" he exulted. "All we're doing is free-booting. We're buccaneers. This is fantastic.

---

[8] Boyd 1992c, *Conceptual Spiral* audio.
[9] Boyd 1977 interview, p. 29.

We can do whatever in the hell we goddamn please. Those generals don't know what the hell we're doing."[10]

In an interview taped after he retired, Boyd describes that mock combat over the Nevada desert in terms that illuminate the unique way his mind worked:

> I would see myself in a vast ball—I would be *inside* the ball—and I could visualize all the actions taking place around the ball [while] all the time of course I am maneuvering.... I could visualize from two reference points. When I was fighting air-to-air, *I could see myself as a detached observer looking at myself, plus all the others around me.*[11]

Unusually, in an American military that believed in regular rotations, Boyd stayed at the Fighter Weapons School for six years, teaching a generation of American and foreign fighter pilots. Meanwhile, he changed the school's emphasis from gunnery (how to shoot) to tactics (how to prevail). He also taught himself calculus at night, and he dictated what would be his only significant print publication. The mimeographed *Aerial Attack Study* was the first attempt to explain air combat maneuvers as an interlinked series of moves and countermoves, one flowing logically into the next.[12] "Within a decade Boyd's [monograph] had become the tactics manual for air forces around the world," writes Jarmo Lindberg of the Finnish Air Force. "It forever changed the way they fought."[13]

And note the title: *Aerial Attack Study*. Boyd expected his pilots always to play offense.

---

[10] Boyd 1992d, *Conceptual Spiral* video.
[11] Boyd 1977 interview (emphasis added).
[12] Boyd 1964, *Aerial Attack Study*. The 1960 original remains classified because it contained information on countering U.S. missiles.
[13] Lindberg 2006, an excellent short take on Boyd's contributions to aerial tactics and fighter design. General Lindberg now commands the Finnish Air Force.

# Energy Manuverability

Typically, if a peacetime Air Force captain hopes to be promoted, he must first earn an advanced degree. But when the education furlough came to John Boyd, he opted instead to study for a second bachelor's degree, this one in industrial engineering at the Georgia Institute of Technology. It was in Atlanta, as a 35-year-old father of five, that a classmate happened to ask what it was that a fighter pilot *did* when he met an enemy aircraft. The questioner was Charles Cooper, an undergraduate little more than half Boyd's age. They were both taking a course in thermodynamics, so Boyd used their common background to explain that, just as a generator can transform mechanical motion into electrical energy, so can a pilot transform higher altitude into greater speed—or either one into the ability to maneuver.

"Then it hit me," as he told the story years later; "Jesus Christ, wait a minute! *I can look at air-to-air combat in terms of energy relationships*. I can lay out equations. I can do it formally now."[14] He spent the rest of the night laying out the equations, and when he was done he had the basis for what would become known as his Energy Maneuverability theory, which the military inevitably shortened to E-M. As he later explained:

> Maneuverability means altitude, airspeed, and direction, in any combination. You can use energy to measure those changes. In other words, *quantify*. Obviously, you can do it for two competing airplanes and some numbers are higher for one airplane over the other.[15]

Just as Boyd's *Aerial Attack Study* caused a revolution in fighter tactics, his E-M theory was "a clear line of demarcation" in aircraft engineering, as his biographer Robert Coram said in a television interview. "It gave a way to quantify the performance of an aircraft, to compare an aircraft['s] performance with that of the adversary, and a way to design aircraft."[16]

Duly promoted, Major Boyd was assigned to Florida's Eglin

---

[14] Boyd 1977 interview, pp. 95-96 (emphasis added).
[15] Ibid, p. 120.
[16] Coram 2003.

Air Force Base, where he continued to plot aircraft performance, develop his E-M graphs, and cultivate the civilian engineers who would design the next-generation fighter aircraft. Among other things, his computer runs correctly predicted that the new and gargantuan F-111 Aardvark, at 114,300 pounds gross weight, would turn out to be inferior in almost every respect to the latest and much lighter Soviet fighters.

Boyd proved to be an inspired briefer, whether speaking to F-105 pilots in Vietnam, to wing commanders in Europe, or—crucially—to the four-star generals charged with procuring future aircraft. He also acquired a not altogether complimentary nickname: the Mad Major. In an argument (and there were many arguments), he famously kept his face three inches from his adversary's, meanwhile tapping the other man's chest with two fingers that held a Dutch Master cigar. On at least two occasions, Boyd supposedly burned a hole in the other man's tie. "Around Eglin," as Robert Coram archly tells us in *Boyd: The Fighter Pilot Who Changed the Art of War*, "he was getting the reputation of a man who might not have both oars in the water."[17]

In his oral history interview, Boyd seems to be saying that he became interested in the German concept of blitzkrieg while working at Eglin, though his biographers would put that study ten years in the future.[18] However that may be, his more pressing concern was to apply his E-M concept to the design of future aircraft. His advocacy was apparently effective, for in 1966 he was transferred to the Pentagon with the mission of developing a fighter to replace the F-105 Thunderchiefs and F-4 Phantoms that were proving inadequate against Russian-built aircraft over North Vietnam.[19]

A puzzling aspect of Boyd's E-M graphs was their clear demonstration that the F-86 Sabre he'd flown in Korea was actually inferior to the MiG-15 used by North Korean and

---

[17] Coram 2002, pp. 138, 180, 226.
[18] Boyd 1977 interview, pp. 91-92, but see Hammond 2001, p. 123; Coram 2002, p. 331; and Osinga 2007, p. 31.
[19] Never mind the hapless F-111 Aardvark, of which six were deployed and three of those mysteriously vanished in Southeast Asia (Fredriksen 1999, p.141).

Chinese pilots. The Russian-built fighter could fly faster, climb higher, turn tighter, and out-accelerate the F-86 ... yet the Americans pilots were credited with a 10:1 victory ratio over their opponents. Even with a healthy discount—fighter pilots, like lesser mortals, often see what they want to see—that was an astonishing outcome. Why did the F-86 prevail? Better training may have accounted for a part, but only a part, of the Americans' edge. "For days," according to Coram, Boyd "went into frequent

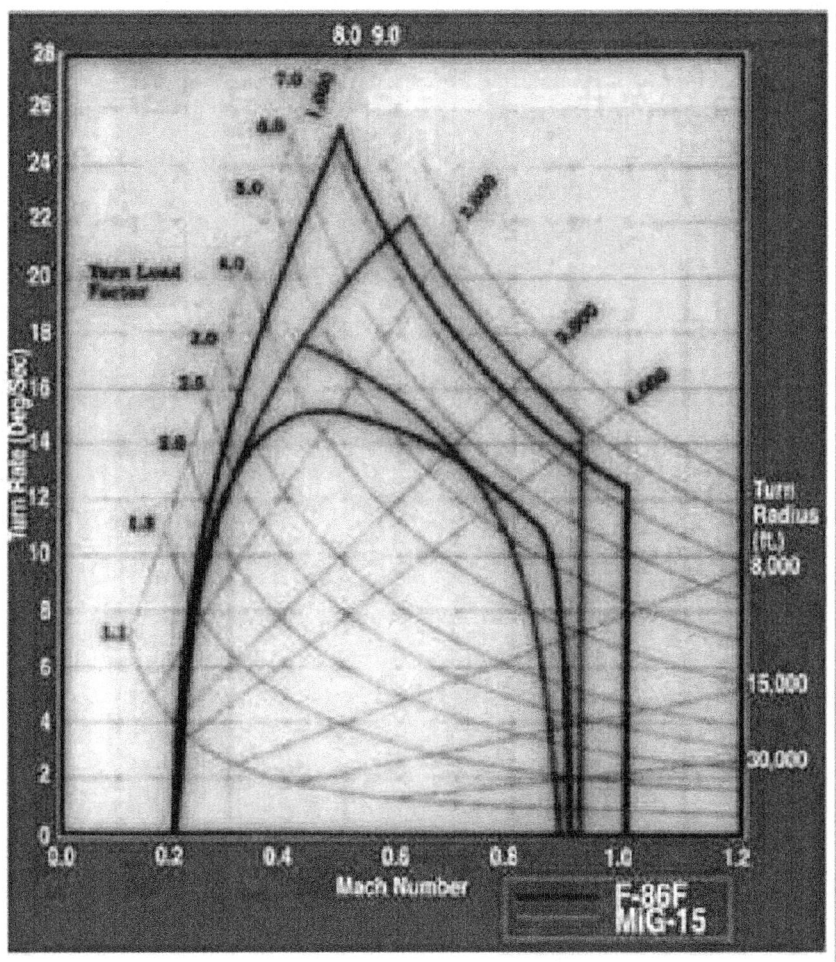

*During the Korean War, as shown in Boyd's E-M graph, the F-86 Sabre was outclassed in almost every respect by the MiG-15. Yet in air-to-air combat it was credited with a 10-1 victory ratio over the enemy fighter (Lindberg 2006).*

trances as he groped for the answer."[20] In the end, he realized that the F-86 had two characteristics that together outweighed the MiG-15's technical superiority. First, the American plane boasted a comparatively clear bubble canopy, contrasted to the old-style Russian canopy with its multiple panes and struts. The American therefore had better "situational awareness," in the pilot's awkward phrase. Given eyesight no better than his opponent's, he could usually spot the MiG before the enemy pilot saw him. Second, the F-86 had fully hydraulic controls that allowed the American to transition faster from one maneuver to another. Boyd would label these advantages *Observation* and *Fast Transients*. The insight led him in time to the OODA Loop— the concept that all combat, indeed all human competition from chess to soccer to business, involves a continuous cycle of Observation, Orientation, Decision, and Action.

## The Fighter Mafia

When he took up his assignment at the Pentagon, Boyd found the Air Force about to commit millions of dollars to designing a fighter that his E-M calculations showed would be "overweight and underwinged, too complex, and far too expensive."[21] With his acolytes—mostly civilian employees—he sweated the behemoth down to a plane whose empty weight was less than half what the Pentagon had intended. "Boyd's E-M theory," writes the Finnish commander Jarmo Lindberg, "made it possible for the first time in fighter design history to analyze the whole maneuvering envelope of a fighter still in design and even prior to the first flight of the prototype."[22] Taken into service as the F-15 Eagle—gross weight 68,000 pounds—the new fighter has served as America's air superiority weapon for more than

---

[20] Coram 2002, p. 255. In Vietnam, too, Russian-built fighters were proving more maneuverable than U.S. fighters (Spinney 1997), in large part because they were lighter. "As marvelous as our [F-4] Phantoms were in air-to-air combat," recalled an American pilot, "they were no match for the MiGs" (Olds et al 2010, p. 314).

[21] Coram 2002, p. 193. Among the bells and whistles was a boarding ladder for the pilot when flying from primitive airfields (p. 205).

[22] Lindberg 2006.

thirty years.

Boyd's group, by now called the Fighter Mafia, followed up with an even smaller aircraft, the F-16 Falcon. Edward Luttwak has complained that scientists and engineers seldom support the development of "diverse, second-best equipment," even though that is often the better policy.[23] The light and cheap F-16 was just such an acquisition. (To be sure, "light" and "cheap" are relative concepts, especially when speaking of Pentagon procurement. The USAF's second-best fighter had a gross weight of 42,300 pounds and cost $10 million a copy.) The F-16 proved to be an ideal multi-role aircraft, and by 2008—thirty-five years after its debut—it was serving in the inventory of twenty-five air forces around the world. Among its admirers is the Dutch scholar-pilot Frans Osinga, who wrote the definitive study of Boyd's intellectual journey, *Science, Strategy and War*. In an email, Colonel Osinga remembers the plane as "wonderfully agile. I was first trained as [an] F-5 pilot and the transition to the F-16 was just mindblowing."[24]

Unique to the aircraft is a thrust-to-weight ratio so great that the pilot can "dump" speed in an increasingly tight turn, forcing a pursuer to shoot past him, then accelerate so quickly that the F-16 is now on the other man's six. This trick is known as the "buttonhook turn," and the F-16 as "the most maneuverable fighter ever designed."[25]

The Fighter Mafia also took up the cause of a third warplane, the ground attack machine that became the A-10 Warthog. Boyd's E-M theory was central to the A-10's development, though he himself had no direct role in the project—nor did he have much empathy for it. "Air-to-ground is bull shit," he explains in his oral history interview. "I just do not feel that I am in control of the situation.... In the air, I can kind of mark the cards."[26] Air Force generals felt much the same way about "air to mud," but

---

[23] Luttwak 1987, p. 29. Boyd might have objected to the reference: "Ed's book was awful," he wrote of Luttwak's "paradoxical logic" of strategy (Boyd Papers, Box 1, folder 10).
[24] Osinga 2009.
[25] Spinney 1997.
[26] Boyd 1977 interview, pp. 59-60.

they wanted the assignment nevertheless. If the USAF didn't build a dedicated attack plane, the ground-support mission would have been flown by U.S. Army warrant officers in a purpose-built assault helicopter.

So Pierre Sprey, one of the civilian members of the Fighter Mafia, was tasked with designing the USAF's first dedicated ground support aircraft—one that could "carry a large payload over a reasonable distance, loiter in the target area for a considerable time, operate under low ceilings in reduced visability [sic] … support troops in contact," and kill enemy tanks.[27] As part of his research, as Sprey told Grant Hammond, he brought German World War II veterans to "CIA safe houses on Maryland's eastern shore" to brief the design team on the air-ground techniques that were central to German battlefield successes in the early years of World War II.[28] However that may be—what need to conceal their assistance, a generation after the war's end, at a time when German engineers were masterminding the American space program?—the team did indeed exploit the Wehrmacht's wartime experience. The briefers included the former tank commanders Hermann Balck and Freidrich von Mellenthin; the dive-bomber pilots Paul-Werner Hozzel and Hans-Ulrich Rudel (the latter credited with destroying 519 enemy tanks); and perhaps the great fighter commander Adolf Galland.[29] Sprey himself was a German speaker, and he assigned a bowdlerized version of Rudel's war diary, called *Stuka Pilot* in translation, as required reading for the design team.[30]

Despite Boyd's aversion to the ground-attack role, the ugly and durable A-10 made a great contribution to the evolution of

---

[27] Ratley 1977, p. 110.
[28] Hammond 2001, p. 121, citing a 1993 interview. Another participant scoffed at this notion: "There was nothing secret about these meetings" (Ratley 2009).
[29] Spinney 2009.
[30] Hammond 2001, p. 121; Coram 2002, p. 235; Campbell 2003, pp. 68-69; Spinney 2009; Rudel 1976. *Stuka* is an abbreviation for *Sturzkampfflugzeug* (dive bomber aircraft) and refers specifically to the Junkers Ju 87. In an amusing twist, the Boyd-inspired F-16 has begun to replace the A-10 for many air–ground missions (Campbell, p. 137).

his thinking. Fascinated by the German military's successes against equivalent or even superior forces through much of World War II, Pierre Sprey urged the older man to make a serious study of the blitzkrieg experience.

# 2 - The OODA Loop

John Boyd almost never published his work, preferring instead to develop his thoughts in briefings that were ever longer and always evolving. "I am verbal [sic] oriented," he explained. Not only did he want the freedom to revise endlessly, but he also enjoyed and profited from the feedback from his audiences.[31] The exceptions were the mimeographed *Aerial Attack Study* of 1960 and the monograph *Destruction and Creation*, completed in 1976.

## Destruction and Creation

He seems to have begun work on the monograph before he retired. As a full colonel, he was deployed to Thailand in 1972 and given command of the 56th Combat Support Group, with the emphasis on *support* rather than *combat*. The assignment gave him time to read and, more important, to think. In August of that year, he wrote his wife Mary that he was "on the verge of a fantastic breakthrough in the thinking processes and how they can be taught to others." And in November: "I may be on the trail of a *theory of learning* quite different and—it appears now—more powerful than methods or theories currently in use."[32]

Boyd was working out the concepts he would eventually distil into an exceedingly dense 3,840 words that he committed to paper in the twelve months following his retirement in August 1975. Paradoxically, *Destruction and Creation* might have been more accessible if he had expanded his thoughts into a book—or, alternatively, reduced them to a set of briefing slides which he would then have presented with the full force of his personality—balancing on the balls of his feet, engaging the audience, and regaling them with anecdotes, analogies, and examples from their shared experience. As it stands, in the words of Robert

---
[31] Boyd 1977 interview, p. 81.
[32] Coram 2002, p. 271, quoting letters dated Aug. 10 and Oct. 15, 1972 (Coram's emphasis).

Coram, the monograph "has a specific gravity approaching that of uranium," while Grant Hammond describes it as "cosmic in its sweep and fundamental in its insight."[33] As befits a Netherlander writing what began as a PhD. dissertation, Colonel Osinga is both more restrained and more informative:

> The heart of the essay is the discussion about the nature of knowledge. It is highly philosophical and obviously rooted in the epistemological debates that raged in the 1960s. Boyd associated these epistemological issues with struggles for survival. *The fundamental, unavoidable and all-pervasive presence of uncertainty is the starting point.* It leads to the requirement to learn, to develop adequate mental models, and to continually assess the adequacy of these models as the basis of survival....[34]

The goal of all human behavior, Boyd begins, is to *increase our capacity for independent action*. We join with others so that we can cooperate—*and compete*—toward that goal. Since the resources available to us are finite, we thereby begin a struggle that can never end. "Against such a background <u>action</u> and <u>decision</u> become critically important," he tells us. If we are to make timely decisions, he continues, "we must be able to form mental concepts of observed reality ... and ... change these concepts as reality itself appears to change."[35]

Each of our mental concepts represents both a *domain* and its *constituent elements*, and we can approach them in two ways, either analytically or deductively. Through analysis, we separate the elements from the domain, an activity that Boyd calls *deductive destruction*. We can then synthesize these disparate elements into "something new and different from what previously existed." Boyd calls this process *constructive induction*. His favorite example of the dual process of destruction and creation is to have his listeners build a mental "snowmobile" by taking elements from the domains of skiing (using only the skis), boating (using the two-cycle outboard engine), motorcycling (the handlebars), and a child's toy tank or earthmover (the treads). To

---

[33] Coram 2002, p. 323; Hammond 2001, p. 120.
[34] Osinga 2007, p. 131 (emphasis added).
[35] Boyd 1976a, *Destruction and Creation*, p. 2. When quoting from the *Discourse*, I underscore words as Boyd did.

be sure, the result must be consistent with observed reality, just as our mental snowmobile resembles the real-life machines sold by Bombardier and Yamaha. "Over and over again," Boyd writes, "this cycle of <u>Destruction</u> and <u>Creation</u> is repeated until we demonstrate internal consistency and match-up with reality."[36]

Yet the correspondence is never entirely complete. Like Achilles pursuing the tortoise in Zeno's paradox, we can keep improving our perception of reality—just as Achilles can get closer to the tortoise—but we can never finally fix it: "Back and forth, over and over again," Boyd writes, "we use observation to sharpen a concept and a concept to sharpen observation." Indeed, he suggests that *the closer we get to the underlying reality, the larger our uncertainty becomes*: "any inward-oriented and continued effort to improve the matchup of concept with observed reality will only increase the degree of mismatch."[37]

We find ourselves in a box, and the only way out is ... to keep thinking outside the box! Again and again, Boyd says, we must "shatter the rigid conceptual pattern" that we have established in our minds: "the process of Structure, Unstructure, and Restructure ... is repeated endlessly in moving to higher and broader levels of elaboration." He concludes his essay by saying, much as he had written to his wife four years earlier: "I believe we have uncovered a Dialectic Engine that permits the construction of decision models needed by individuals and societies for determining and monitoring actions ... to cope with their environment—or to improve their capacity for independent action."[38]

## Fast Transients

Simultaneously with *Destruction and Creation*, Boyd developed a briefing entitled *New Conception for Air-to-Air*

---

[36] Ibid, p. 7. Boyd 1992b recasts the theory as the *Conceptual Spiral*. For the "snowmobile," see Boyd 1992d, *Conceptual Spiral* Q&A.
[37] Ibid, pp. 10, 13. Here Boyd is playing off Werner Heisenberg's "Uncertainty Principle" (see footnote 57).
[38] Ibid, pp. 14, 15, 16.

*Combat*, more commonly known as *Fast Transients*. Oddly, this "brief" doesn't get much attention in the Boyd canon, though it seems to be the first explication of his iconic theory of the OODA Loop. In it, Boyd is still concerned mostly with the performance of fighter aircraft. Manuverability, as he notes on an early slide, is the *"ability to change altitude, airspeed and direction in any combination."*[39] Like so many of Boyd's ideas, this is a deceptively simple formulation, and one that, to the best of my knowledge, he was the first to advance.

More important than the *fact* of change, he goes on, is the *speed* of change, as illustrated by the F-16's dazzling "buttonhook turn." It is the fast transient that enables the lightweight fighter to perform better than its E-M profile predicted, much as the F-86 of the Korean War was able to outmaneuver its technically superior opponent. Better yet, Boyd argues, what matters most is the *tempo* of change: "fast transients suggests that—in order to win or gain superiority—we should operate at a faster tempo than our adversaries or inside our adversaries['] time scales." Clearly, Boyd has already begun his obsessive study of military history. The very next slide gives three examples of tempo, and only one of them involves air-to-air combat: the German invasion of France in May 1940; the F-86 Sabre vs. the MiG-15 during the Korean War; and the Israeli rescue of a hijacked airliner at Entebbe, Uganda, in July 1976.[40]

In short, Boyd's "new conception" of air-to-air combat asks the pilot to exploit his environment and his aircraft's technical features in order to "Generate a rapidly changing environment (quick/clear observations, fast tempo, fast transients, quick kill)." But that's not nearly enough. At the same time, the pilot must strive to suppress or distort his opponent's observations, thus inhibiting his ability to adapt to the changing environment. The goal is to "unstructure" the opponent's "system," reducing him to "confusion and disorder," so that he over-reacts and under-reacts to the situation "because of activity that appears uncertain, ambiguous or chaotic." The brief's final message: *"He*

---

[39] Boyd 1976b, *New Conception*, slide 6 (emphasis added); Spinney 1997.
[40] Ibid, slides 19, 20.

*who can handle the quickest rate of change survives.*"[41] Here is OODA without the Loop.

With respect to the dogfights of the Korean War, Boyd now has a tool to explain the anomaly in his E-M graphs. The F-86 Sabre's fully powered hydraulic controls were easier to handle than the hydraulically boosted controls on the MiG-15; though the American fighter had a larger (hence more vulnerable) radius of turn, it was quicker from one freeze-frame moment to the next. As a result, in the words of one of Boyd's acolytes, Chuck Spinney, "an F-86 that was losing the fight—with a MiG about 40 degrees [off] his tail—could start a turn in one direction, then, as the MiG followed, reverse the turn.... The maneuver might gain the F-86 pilot 10 degrees almost immediately, putting the MiG 50 degrees off." Repeated changes of direction "would put the MiG pilot farther and farther out of sequence: relatively quickly, the F-86 pilot would be able to work himself into an advantageous firing position."[42] Not only was the American pilot quicker to transition; he expended less physical effort in doing so, enabling him to exhaust his opponent even as he drove him to the edge of panic. (Russian pilots were known to spend their off-duty hours lifting weights, to develop the upper-body strength required of a MiG pilot.) The result was the 10:1 victory ratio that so puzzled Boyd when he calculated E-M curves for the two aircraft.

A year after the *Fast Transients* brief, he sat down with Lieutenant Colonel John Dick at Maxwell Air Force Base, Alabama, for the oral history interview that would review his military career. At 250 manuscript pages, the interview in effect is the book that Boyd never wrote. In it, he explains the concept of fast transients by talking the colonel through an OODA Loop, though Boyd hasn't yet hit upon that term. In his Socratic manner, he proposes that the two men are engaged in a dogfight. Boyd always liked to put himself in the position of his interlocutor, so he lets the colonel have the advantage—in effect, Colonel Dick gets the white queen and Boyd takes the black. Early in their hypothetical contest, Boyd makes a feint, but he postulates that it is a weak one:

---

[41] Ibid, slides 22, 24 (emphasis added).
[42] Spinney 1997.

That did not work so good. I have to make another adjustment. *We go through the loop again....* Your rhythm is inside my rhythm.... I am going to tend to become a bit uncertain because your actions appear ambiguous to me ... and pretty soon I am confused, disordered, and going into a panic situation.

In much the same way, he goes on to explain, the Germans operated inside the Anglo-French rhythm in May 1940. The French did indeed panic ("hallucinate" is the word Boyd uses, quoting a contemporary account), just as his theory predicts. For their part, the Germans did indeed feel a rhythm to their advance, and what's more they reported that *their rhythm seemed faster than the enemy's*. "So the external manifestations support it [the theory]," Boyd concludes.[43]

## On Winning and Losing

Soon after talking to Colonel Dick, Boyd diagrammed the OODA Loop for the first time, and he gave it the name by which it became famous.[44] He would spend the rest of his life refining it, as he did with the increasingly elaborate briefings that he eventually assembled into his magnum opus, *A Discourse on Winning and Losing*.[45] As a briefing book, the *Discourse* comes to 370 pages, most of them slides intended for projection and oral explication. As a presentation, the *Discourse* could occupy as many as fifteen hours over the course of two days. Even the early versions were exhausting: "At the end of four hours," complained a faculty member at the U.S. Army Command and Staff College, "I was ready for oxygen, not questions."[46]

After he retired in 1975, Boyd continued his studies on his own and as a nominally paid consultant to the U.S. Department of Defense. He soon came to the conclusion that all stages of

---

[43] Boyd 1977 interview, pp. 134, 139, 140 (emphasis added). This typescript was sent to Boyd for his approval, and it contains his handwritten corrections and additions.
[44] Watts 1995.
[45] Boyd 1992a, *Discourse*.
[46] Boyd Papers, Box 5, folder 8 (statement by Associate Professor Roger Spiller).

the OODA Loop are not created equal. Orientation, he decided, is the *schwerpunkt*—one of his favorite terms, as it was a favorite of Clausewitz's, and likewise of the advocates of the 21st Century doctrine of maneuver warfare. The schwerpunkt is the decisive point in any endeavor—the focus of effort—the center of gravity. For Clausewitz and later German theorists, it is the place at which a military operation should be directed, typically the weakest point in the enemy's line. For Boyd, it identifies the decisive point of the OODA Loop and indeed of all human decision-making:

> • Orientation is the schwerpunkt. It shapes the way we interact with the environment—hence orientation shapes the way we <u>observe</u>, the way we <u>decide</u>, the way we <u>act</u>.
>
> In this sense
>
> • Orientation shapes the character of <u>present</u> observation-orientation-decision-action loops—while these present loops shape the character of <u>future</u> orientation.[47]

As the warfighter orients himself (and this is the crucial point), he brings to the process not only the imperatives of his immediate situation—whether piloting an F-86 over the Yalu River, leading an armored column through the Ardennes Forest, or planning the invasion of Iraq—but all his past experiences and the values of the society in which he was raised. "What a man sees," in the words of Thomas Kuhn, "depends both upon what he looks at and also upon what his previous visual-conceptual experience has taught him to see."[48] Indeed, Boyd argues, Orientation is nothing less than "the interplay of <u>genetic heritage, cultural tradition, previous experiences</u>, and <u>unfolding circumstances</u>."[49] Only the last of these is normally considered by the warfighter, chess player, or businessman trying to get an edge on his immediate adversary, or indeed by most commentators writing about John Boyd's philosophy.

---

[47] Boyd 1987a, *Organic Design*, slide 16 (emphasis original). Despite the date, the briefing and probably the phrasing would have taken shape years before.
[48] Kuhn 1962, p. 112.
[49] Boyd 1987a, *Organic Design*, slide 15.

Nor are the relationships between Observation, Orientation, Decision, and Action limited to "feed forward," as the Loop is usually diagrammed, neatly advancing through the four stages of the cycle. (By so doing, they fall into the same trap as Clausewitz with his closed triad of Strategy, Planning, and Tactics.) Rather, there is feed*back* at every stage of the cycle. By this time, too, Boyd in his sketches has made a plural out of the Observation stage of the cycle.[50] There are many observations, not just one.

Meanwhile, Boyd's acolytes were expanding his theories into the concept of Fourth Generation Warfare, most significantly in a 1989 article published simultaneously (and unusually) in the *Marine Corps Gazette* and the U.S. Army's *Military Review*.[51] The article was "one of the first, if not *the* first, attempt to understand how modern warfare was actually changing" from orderly clashes between roughly equivalent state actors to decentralized bloodletting, in which the sponsorship and even identity of one's assailant may be unknown."[52] Indeed, after the terrorist attacks of 9/11, the article seemed so prescient (the authors warned, for example, that "some non-Western areas, such as the Islamic world, ... [might] develop a fourth generation through ideas rather than technology"[53]) that the Marine journal republished it in November 2001.

Arguably, the first real-world application of the OODA Loop came in the 1991 Gulf War. General Norman Swartzkopf's initial war plan—"high diddle diddle, straight up the middle"—was vetoed by then-Secretary of Defense Richard Cheney in favor of deception and maneuver, including a feint by the U.S. Marines to persuade the Iraqis that an amphibious landing was about to occur. During the run-up to the war, Cheney seems to have been regularly briefed by Boyd, and in an interview with C-SPAN's Brian Lamb, Robert Coram credits him as the architect of the American victory:

> LAMB: What part of the [1991] Gulf war ... plan did John Boyd have some responsibility for?

---

[50] Boyd 1996, slide 4.
[51] Lind et al 1989.
[52] Hammes 2005.
[53] Lind et al 1989.

CORAM: All of it. The multiple thrust[s], the feints, the ambiguity, the Marine thrust, the ...

LAMB: You mean the landing in Kuwait, the early landing?

CORAM: Yes. Yes.

LAMB: That was his idea?

CORAM: It was his idea. He was behind all of it.[54]

An army spokesman afterward explained the swift coalition victory in explicitly Boydian language, saying of the Iraqi enemy, "We kind of *got inside his decision cycle*."[55] Similarly, after the 2003 invasion of Iraq, General Tommy Franks explained the victory this way: "And that is the business of decision cycles, or *inside the decision loop*, as people say ... if, in fact, you can deceive him with respect to what you're going to do, to cause him further confusion and make him keep his force in place one day too long, then, in fact, you may find yourself all the way to Baghdad."[56]

So the OODA Loop has become the conventional shorthand, without the need to credit it beyond an offhand "as people say."

## Toward a more expansive Loop

John Boyd's archived papers at the Gray Research Center in Quantico, Virginia, contain multiple iterations of the *Discourse* and the OODA Loop, as he kneaded and pummelled and tested them over the years. Late in 1992, he sketched a particularly interesting Loop, a portion of which is reproduced nearby (see the full sketch online at www.danford.net/boyd/ooda.htm). Here Boyd is playing with the notion that a scientist grappling with a problem goes through roughly the same mental processes as a fighter pilot bounced by an enemy aircraft.

---

[54] Coram 2003, in which he recalls an interview with then Vice-President Cheney confirming one session with Boyd. Also see Coram 2002, pp. 422-24.
[55] Coram 2002, p. 425 (emphasis added).
[56] Boyer 2003 (emphasis added).

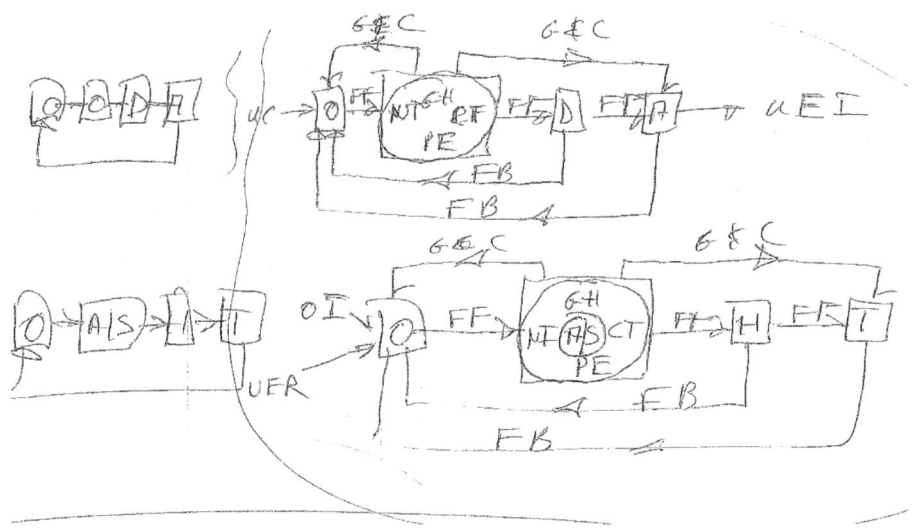

*Here Boyd sketches how a scientist orients himself through new information (gained in observation) filtered through his genetic heritage, his cultural traditions, and his previous experiences.*

Each begins with an observation—he sees the situation as it exists. The pilot (or soldier or footballer or chess or tennis player) then moves on to orientation, though in a manner much more complex than the OODA Loop is usually understood. In the popular view, the combatant simply orients himself with respect to the *new information* (*NI*, as Boyd abbreviates it on the sketch) that observation has revealed to him. As noted above, Boyd has earlier used what seems to me to be a more evocative term, *unfolding circumstances*, which makes the point that the process is a fluid one. This is a rare instance in which Boyd's obsessive rewriting has actually made his meaning less clear.

But orientation has only begun. The combatant also filters the new information (or unfolding circumstances) through the lenses of his *previous experiences* (*PE*, in Boyd's sketch), his *genetic heritage* (*GH*), and his *cultural traditions* (*CT*). On this basis, he decides what he must do. Then he acts upon his decision. So we have the combatant's OODA Loop: *Observation > Orientation > Decision > Action*.

For the scientist, Boyd speculates, the opening observation is processed in a somewhat different manner, which he terms

*Synthesis / Analysis*, though it involves the same galaxy of forces as the combatant applies in the orientation stage of his OODA Loop. (And here, I suspect, Boyd is thinking of Thomas Kuhn's theory of the "paradigm" as part of the scientist's cultural tradition. Kuhn argued that certain basic assumptions govern every era's ruling theory of science, until the paradigm changes and a new set of assumptions replaces them. As with Werner Heisenberg's Uncertainty Principle and Kurt Gödel's eponymous "Proof," Boyd was much taken by Kuhn's formulation of the Paradigm Shift, and he returns to these ideas again and again in his briefings.[57]) Based on the insights gained in that process, the scientist then formulates a *Hypothesis* and subjects it to *Test*, thus completing his own, analogous Loop. No less than aerial combat, science turns out to be "a self-correcting process of observations, analysis / synthesis, hypothesis, and test."[58]

Toward the end of his life, in a briefing at Maxwell's Air War College, Boyd explained the genesis of the OODA Loop, as a metaphorical snowmobile constructed out of his encounters with Heisenberg, Gödel, and Kuhn, and those in turn layered onto his thermodynamics course at Georgia Tech. Nothing in life, he told the young officers, is certain. "If that's true, what those people wanted to do in the 19th Century, you can't do. *You're not going to nail things down....* Some things we can predict, other things we can't.... The non-linear stuff totally overwhelms the linear.... The rational is swimming in a sea of the irrational." He goes on to complete the "snowmobile" with elements from his Energy Maneuverability theory and his years of teaching aerial combat at Nellis Air Force Base:

> And it occurred to me ... that if I have an adversary out there, that what I want to do is fold my adversary back inside himself, where he can't really consult the external environment he has to deal with.... *Then I can drive him into confusion and disorder and bring*

---

[57] Thomas Kuhn, *The Structure of Scientific Revolutions* ; Werner Heisenberg, *Physics and Philosophy*; and Ernest Nagel and James Newman, *Gödel's Proof*, are among the works cited in the bibliography for Boyd's *Destruction and Creation* (p. B-2). Also see Osinga 2007, p. 56.

[58] Boyd 1992c, *Conceptual Spiral* audio. Some of the scientist / warfighter analogies are incorporated in Boyd 1996, slide 4.

> *about paralysis....* If I can operate at a tempo or rhythm faster than he can operate at—well, he can't keep up with me, and in effect then I fold him back inside himself. And if I do that—ball game! You saw it in Desert Storm, you see it in basketball games, football games, and a whole bunch of other stuff.[59]

The warrior's object, then, is to create "pandemonium, chaos, disorder—and you sweep out the debris."

> We want to get inside another guy's tempo or rhythm, where we pull him down.... We gotta get an image or picture in our head, which we call orientation. Then we have to make a decision as to what we're going to do, and then implement the decision.... Then we look at the [resulting] action, plus our observation, and we drag in new data, new orientation, new decision, new action, ad infinitum.... Orientation isn't just a state you're in; it's a process. *You're always orienting....*

> A nice tight little world where there's no change—[creatures who live in such a world are] dinosaurs; they're going to die. The name of the game is not to become a dinosaur.... If you're in an equilibrium condition, you're dead.... The underlying message is simple: *there is no way out....* That's the way it is, guys.[60]

"Boyd's corpus is remarkably slight," according to Lawrence Freedman in a review of Frans Osinga's *Science, Strategy and War*. "His most famous idea turns out to have been over-simple. His military history was often suspect."[61] The first complaint is certainly true, if published books are the measure of a scholar, and the final one may have some validity. But ... *over-simple?* One wonders if Sir Lawrence has actually looked at the "corpus."

His easy dismissal of the OODA Loop seems as commonplace in the academy as is the fevered admiration of Boyd's acolytes. I find only two scholars who speak kindly of him. Writing of modern strategists worthy to follow in Clausewitz's footsteps, Colin Gray concludes: "The OODA loop may appear too humble to merit categorization as grand theory, but that is what it is. It has an elegant simplicity, an extensive domain of applicability, and contains a high quality of insight about strategic

---

[59] Boyd 1992c, *Conceptual Spiral* audio (emphasis added).
[60] Ibid.
[61] Freedman 2007.

essentials, such that its author merits honourable mention as an outstanding general theorist of strategy."[62] Similarly, Antoine Bousquet regards Boyd as "a crucial pivotal figure in the emergence of scientifically inspired military thought."[63] And Bruce Berkowitz (like Edward Luttwak, more of a "public intellectual" than an academic) gives Boyd a somewhat muted tribute, calling him "probably the most important military thinker the public has never heard of."[64]

Yet outside the academy, Boyd has become something of a cult figure. A manual on *Maneuver Warfare* cites his name thirty-six times; there's an occasional Boyd Conference in the United States or Canada; and several websites and books are devoted largely to promoting his ideas. Of these last, all are laudatory, and Robert Coram's biography takes it to the extreme. Boyd, he declares, "was the greatest military theoretician since Sun Tzu," thus vaulting him not only past Admiral Mahan, but also past the great Clausewitz himself. As for Boyd's E-M theory of air combat, Coram regards it "as fundamental and as significant to aviation as Newton was to physics."[65]

One point that should be stressed: the OODA Loop is not a speed competition, as it is too often misrepresented. Even less is it a simple four-step process that ends with the combatant's action. A retired Marine Corps officer has described the concept thus:

> Under OODA loop theory every combatant *observes* the situation, *orients* himself, ... *decides* what to do and then *does it*. If his opponent can do this faster, however, his own actions become outdated and disconnected to the true situation, and his opponent's advantage increases geometrically. The [1915-1945] German army's deliberate sacrifice of centralized control to gain

---

[62] Gray 1999, p. 91. In a later work, however, he is more skeptical of the OODA Loop (Gray 2006, pp. 192, 204).
[63] Bousquet 2009, p. 187. Note that Freedman, Gray, and Bousquet are each affiliated with a British university. American scholars are more likely to ignore Boyd altogether.
[64] Berkowitz 2003.
[65] Coram 2002, pp. 445, 127.

faster OODA loops produced many tactical and operational successes against numerically superior opponents.[66]

Alas, to list the elements of the Loop is to oversimplify it, because as with the Clausewitzian triad of Strategy > Planning > Tactics, it implies that the Loop stops after a single revolution. To the contrary, the resulting *action* leads inevitably to a new *observation*, so the cycle runs again and again until the contest breaks off or one side is defeated. And what is true of the fighter pilot is true as well of the general staff, and even of the warring nation or coalition of nations. As Boyd himself explained to the House Armed Services Committee in April 1991: "Conflict can be viewed as repeated cycles of observing-orienting-deciding-acting by both sides (and at all levels)." Unfortunately, he then went on to say: "The adversary that can move through these cycles faster gains an inestimable advantage by disrupting his enemy's ability to respond effectively."[67]

Speed is certainly important, and it provides a convenient shorthand for discussing the OODA Loop. Robert Coram, for example, said much the same thing in a television interview: "if you can cycle through the loop quicker than an adversary, you cause ambiguity, confusion, mistrust in his mind.... So you're getting inside his decision cycle, and he becomes confused. He turns inward instead of outward. He mentally collapses."[68] But speed alone doesn't produce that outcome. In *Patterns of Conflict*, Boyd takes care to emphasize this: our actions, he says, must be "more subtle, more indistinct, more irregular, and quicker—*yet appear to be otherwise.*"[69]

The OODA Loop, like the *Aerial Attack Study* and E-M theory, has been adopted by militaries around the world. "Every self-respecting briefing on [Command and Control] issues has a reference to it," writes the Swedish officer Berndt Brehmer, who notes that his own army's 2002 *Militärstrategisk doktrin* uses the

---

[66] Sayen 2008.
[67] Ibid.
[68] Coram 2003.
[69] Boyd 1986, *Patterns of Conflict*, slide 175 (emphasis added).

OODA Loop.[70] During the 1990s, the debt to Boyd tended to be explicit, as in the 1985 *Maneuver Warfare Handbook*—written by a civilian but intended for the U.S. Marines—which speaks of "Boyd Cycling the enemy."[71] Similarly, the Pentagon's 1996 *Joint Vision* document stresses the need to gain "OODA-loop dominance" on the battlefield.[72] More recently, the tendency is to use only Boyd's language, without attribution, as when the *British Defence Doctrine* speaks of "attack[ing] the enemy commander's decision process by [getting] inside his decision making cycle."[73]

To a remarkable extent, the OODA Loop has become the conventional wisdom for writers about any sort of conflict—on the battlefield, in the marketplace, or in the sports arena. Thus Colonel Thomas Hammes can write: "In Kosovo, the seizure of UN hostages was *the first step of a cycle*. The media was then used to transmit images of them chained to a bridge. Then the insurgents watched TV to determine the response of the various governments [before settling on their next step] ... *much faster than the bureaucratic reporting processes of NATO could complete the same cycle.*"[74] In short, the insurgents got inside NATO's OODA Loop.

---

[70] Brehmer 2005.
[71] Lind 1985 p. 6.
[72] Quoted in Osinga 2007, p. 5.
[73] Osinga 2007, p. 4.
[74] Hammes 2005 (emphasis added).

# 3 - Of blitzers and guerrillas

In retirement, Boyd at first supported himself, his wife, and their five children on his monthly pension of $1,344, the better to devote himself to his studies. (Like his sister, one of Boyd's children was afflicted with polio.) Later he became a consultant at the Pentagon for the sake of the office supplies, telephones, copy machines, and travel expenses the job would provide him. He supposedly worked without salary for the first few years, then for the smallest sum permitted by Pentagon rules: one day's pay in each two-week period. His parsimonious lifestyle earned him a new nickname: the Ghetto Colonel. "Boyd knew he had to be independent," Robert Coram says of the colonel's retirement, "and he saw only two ways for a man to do this: he can either achieve great wealth or reduce his needs to zero. Boyd said if a man can reduce his needs to zero, he is truly free: there is nothing that can be taken from him and nothing anyone can do to hurt him."[75]

Boyd's near-monastic existence stands in ironic contrast to his 21st Century popularity among business writers, both academics and popularizers. I find him quoted, for example, in a tome devoted to strategies for coping with the Sarbanes-Oxley Act of 2002, which imposed onerous reporting requirements on U.S. corporations in the wake of the Enron collapse the previous year.[76]

## Blitzkrieg

As Pierre Sprey had urged, Boyd began his study of military history with the blitzkrieg campaigns that had astounded and demoralized Europe in September 1939, May 1940, and July 1941. In a few months of combat—first against Poland; then against Holland, Belgium, France, and a British expeditionary force; and finally against Russia—Germany accomplished what it

---
[75] Coram 2002, p. 319; also pp. 318, 340.
[76] Quartermain 2006, pp. 73, 86, 87, 143. Also see Richards 2004.

had so signally failed to do in 1914-1918, and at a comparatively low cost. The Battle of France left 156,000 Germans killed, wounded, or captured, as compared to nearly a million Allied casualties (more than two million if we count the French soldiers taken to Germany as forced laborers). As for the invasion of the Soviet Union, though a strategic disaster, it was rewarded in the early years by "the largest and most spectacular victories in the history of land warfare," in the words of Stephen Bungay.[77]

Blitzkrieg—or "manuever warfare," as we call it now that Germany's former enemies have embraced it—would become Boyd's great interest, in contrast to the attritional or "industrial" combat that began with Napoleon's *Levée en masse* and that ended for us, or so we fondly hope, in August 1945 with the obliteration of Hiroshima and Nagasaki. (It did not end, however, for the non-nuclear powers. The Iran-Iraq War of 1980-1988 resembled World War I more than any other, even to trench warfare and mustard gas.) For Boyd, Carl von Clausewitz was the unholy drummer whose beat accompanied two centuries of brutal conflict between nations in arms, as he characterized it in *Patterns of Conflict*:

> ... tactical regularity and the continued use of large stereotyped formations for tactical assaults, together with the mobilization of large armies and massing of enormous supplies through a narrow logistical network, "telegraphed" any punch hence minimized the possibility of exploiting ambiguity, deception, and mobility to generate surprise for a decisive edge.[78]

The consequence of this thinking was the stupendous bloodletting of Leipzig (1813), Gettysburg (1863), the Somme (1916), and Stalingrad (1942-1943), the last of which claimed the lives, health, or freedom of perhaps two million soldiers and civilians. Boyd arguably is too ready to accept the stereotype of Clausewitz as "an unwavering strategist of annihilation," as one observer puts it.[79] In fact, the two men are not really that far apart in their thinking. Like the American colonel, the Prussian general emphasizes what he knew best, in his case the clash of national

---

[77] Bungay 2005.
[78] Boyd 1986, *Patterns of Conflict*, slide 49.
[79] Fadok 1995, p. 5.

armies. Yet *On War* also contains a chapter devoted to irregular combat—what Clausewitz called "The People in Arms"—and the success of the Spanish guerrillas who supported the British Army during the Peninsular War (1808-1814).[80]

It was to escape the meat grinder of industrial-scale warfare that the Germans experimented in 1918 with *Stoßtruppen* (storm troopers) and the Italians with their *Arditi* ("the daring").[81] Though able to break through enemy lines and sow local disorder, these elite units proved too "light" to change the course of a campaign. The real breakthrough took place in 1939-1941, when the Wehrmacht scaled up the storm-trooper concept to the armored column, supported it with dive bombers, and tied them together with two-way radio communication, thus creating the immensely successful combined-arms assaults that became known as blitzkrieg.

Blitzkrieg, in John Keegan's useful formulation, is "a doctrine of attack on a narrow front by concentrated armor, trained to drive forward through the gap it forced without concern for its flanks."[82] The key is not so much the armor, nor even motorization (the Wehrmacht had fewer tanks and trucks in May 1940 than did the Anglo-French forces), but the concentration of force—on a *narrow* front, as Keegan notes, but more important on a *weak* part of the front. Thus the advance through Belgium's seemingly impenetrable Ardennes Forest, avoiding both the fortified Maginot Line to the south and the Allied armies defending Belgium on the north. Once a breakthrough was effected, the tanks rampaged through the enemy's rear area, spreading panic, confusion, and eventual paralysis.

To Boyd, these German innovations seemed more familiar than not. In his studies, he had worked backward from the World War II German tank commander Heinz Guderian to the Chinese theorist Sun-tzu. Though he borrowed generously from more modern thinkers—Basil Liddell Hart and J. F. C Fuller; Robert E. Lee and T. E. Lawrence—no one was more important to him than the possibly apocryphal "Master Sun" who applied the

---
[80] Clausewitz 1976, pp. 479-483.
[81] Ortmann 2009.
[82] Keegan 1987, p. 259.

philosophy of Taoism to *The Art of War* some 2,500 years ago. More than simply a source, he was "Boyd's conceptual father."[83] In Ralph Sawyer's translation, Sun advises military commanders to strike where they are not expected:

> Warfare is the Way (Tao) of deception. Thus although [you are] capable, display incapability toward them. When committed to deploying your forces, feign inactivity. When [your objective] is nearby, make it appear as if distant....
>
> Create disorder in their ranks, and take them.
>
> If they are substantial, prepare for them; if they are strong, avoid them....
>
> If they are united, cause them to be separated.
>
> Attack where they are unprepared.
>
> Go forth where they will not expect it.
>
> These are the ways military strategists are victorious.[84]

Just so, when the German armored columns crashed through the Ardennes Forest in May 1940, they were going forth where the Anglo-French commanders did not expect them; and in their dash to the Channel, they caused the Allied armies to be separated. Even more disorienting, in Sun-tzu's simile, the German tanks flowed "like water" through gaps in the Allied lines. General Heinz Guderian thus executed in steel and fire the Chinese philosopher's charming prescription: "The army's disposition of force *(hsing)* avoids the substantial and attacks the vacuous."[85] Consequently, he was victorious. ("Vacuous" is a somewhat misleading translation. More useful to the soldier is the notion of a void, gap, or fissure in the enemy's lines.[86])

Boyd loves this notion, and on a slide he diagrams how a "blitzer" advances, in multiple, jagged, multi-pronged thrusts, first

---

[83] Osinga 2007, p. 35.
[84] Sun-tzu 1994, p. 168 (brackets in the original). Much as happened with John Boyd, Sun-tzu has become the darling of writers on business strategy.
[85] Ibid, p. 193.
[86] Sawyer 2007, p. 68. Sun-tzu's translator has written a useful exposition of the Chinese way of war. See especially Chapter Three.

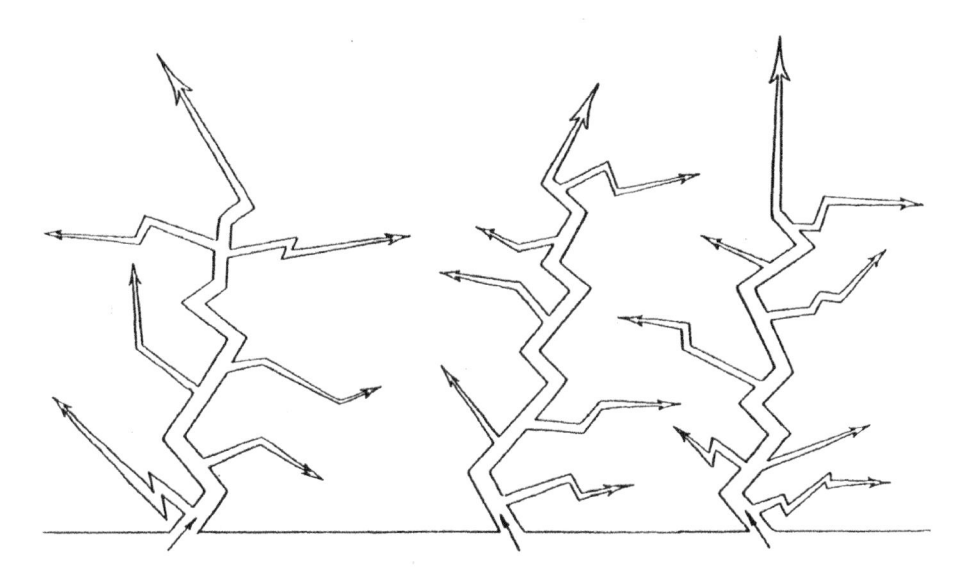

*Blitzkrieg: "Armored assault teams ... quickly open breaches ... into adversary rear along paths of least resistance"*
*(Boyd 1986,* Patterns of Conflict, *slide 80).*

finding the weak spots in the enemy's defenses, then penetrating them. In prose as jagged as his depiction of a blitzkrieg advance, Boyd's briefing slides describe how the German military exploited bottom-up communication and decision making in order to operate inside the enemy's OODA Loop. As he explains in *Patterns of Conflict*, his 185-slide survey of warfare from the Battle of Marathon to World War II:

> The German operational philosophy based upon a common outlook and freedom-of-action, and realized through their concepts of mission and schwerpunkt, emphasized <u>implicit over explicit</u> communication.

which suggests

> The secret of the German Command and Control System lies in what's <u>unstated or not communicated to one another</u>—in order to exploit lower-level initiative yet realize higher-level intent, thereby diminish friction and reduce time, hence gain both quickness and security.

Result

The Germans were able to repeatedly operate inside their adversary's observation-orientation-decision-action loops.[87]

Here Boyd is describing what is now called "mission command," a free translation of the German *Auftragstaktik*. He prefers the German word and regularly employs it and similar terms in his briefings.

## Mission command

Auftragstaktik was not new to the German army in 1939, or even in 1918. "Senior commanders should 'not order more than is absolutely necessary' but should ensure that the goal was clear," as Stephen Bungay summarizes the *Field Service Regulations* of 1869, authored in large part by Field Marshal von Moltke. "In case of doubt, subordinate commanders should seize the initiative."[88] The concept—often neglected in the intervening years—would be refined in the *Troop Leadership* manual of 1933:

> The basis of leadership is to be found in the task (*Auftrag*) and the situation. They must constantly be held in view.... *Uncertainty of the situation is the rule*.... When the plan no longer corresponds to the situation, or if it is obviated by events, so must the plan take these facts into consideration.... In the changing fortunes of war, however, to hold stubbornly to a decision regardless of the situation may amount to a fault.... A commander must give his subordinates a free hand in execution so far as it does not endanger his objective.[89]

Auftragstaktik gave the German military in World War II—and not just the ground forces—a remarkable ability to adapt to changing circumstances. The tactical success of the Wehrmacht is often attributed to the brilliance of German generals, as when Edward Luttwak speaks of Erwin Rommel's advance into Libya in April 1941: "With Rommel leading them in person, the Germans could act much faster than the British, much as a

---

[87] Boyd 1986, *Patterns of Conflict*, slide 79 (emphasis original).
[88] Bungay 2005.
[89] Quoted in Bungay 2005 (emphasis added).

better fighter pilot ... can turn inside the circle of a more sluggish opponent ... *while his opponent is still trying to react to the first turn.*"[90] Luttwak is channelling John Boyd, while missing the crucial fact that it was not so much Rommel as Auftragstaktik that let the Afrika Korps operate inside the OODA Loop of the British 8th Army.

Boyd himself defined the German system as "a contract, hence an agreement, between superior and subordinate. The subordinate agrees to make his actions serve his superior's intent in terms of <u>what</u> is to be accomplished, while the superior agrees to give his subordinate wide freedom to exercise his imagination and initiative in terms of <u>how</u> intent is to be realized."[91]

"I always prized most highly those commanders that needed to be given the least orders," said Hermann Balck of crossing the river Meuse in May 1940—"those you could discuss the matter with for five minutes and then not worry about them for the next eight days." His superiors were equally laconic: "when we reached the Meuse," Balck recalled, "the only order we got from division was, 'Proceed as in the war [games] at Koblenz'."[92] Carl Builder and his colleagues describe the result:

> Guderian's XIX Panzer [Tank] Corps crossed the Meuse on the fly, straight from the march. After an intense bombardment of the river defenses by the Luftwaffe, lasting nearly the entire day, elements of the 1st Panzer Division, led by Lieutenant-Colonel Hermann Balck's 1st Panzer Grenadier Regiment, managed to cross and establish a toehold on the west bank of the Meuse ... during the early evening hours of May 14.[93]

Much the same was true of the air force. "Local commanders had the authority to conduct operations as they saw fit," recalled Hans-Ulrich Rudel of his dive-bomber squadrons. "Individual units were given assignments and how they carried it out was

---

[90] Luttwak 1987, p. 213 (emphasis added).
[91] Boyd 1986, *Patterns of Conflict*, slide 76.
[92] Balck 1979, pp. 26, 4. Boyd cited this and other interviews of German veterans in the bibliography of *Patterns of Conflict* (Boyd 1986, slides 192-93).
[93] Builder et al 1999.

generally their business."[94] Similarly, pilots refueling at an advanced field would continue the combat under the leadership of the senior officer present, rather than return to their home station as American or British pilots would have done.

What astounded the world in the early years of World War II has since become the conventional wisdom. "Today," concludes Stephen Bungay, "the operational manuals of organisations like the U.S. Marine Corps or the British Army all contain passages which could have been lifted from the [*Troop Leadership* manual]."[95]

## Infiltration tactics

As Grant Hammond points out, Boyd does not make it easy for the reader to trace the development of his thought. "Not being academically trained," Hammond writes, "Boyd did not properly cite [quotations] from others. Where possible, I have tried to do so; however, the number of citations from Marx and Lenin and the voluminous writings of each has made this difficult, if not impossible."[96]

Boyd had earned two undergraduate degrees, but the first seems not to have amounted to much. (The University of Iowa was a "corn college," he supposedly said of his first bout with higher education; "I got nothing out of it."[97]) His second undergraduate program, in engineering at Georgia Tech, was considerably more fruitful, but it provided no great experience in academic research and writing. He therefore followed the autodidact's route of diving into his subject at hazard, beginning with blitzkrieg and working back to Sun-tzu. He read voraciously, often in secondary sources and in periodicals, underlining and making marginal notes as he went. If he kept a document in his files, or if he made a machine copy of the part that interested

---

[94] Rudel 1976.
[95] Bungay 2005.
[96] Hammond 2001, p. 224.
[97] Coram 2002, p. 34. Unfortunately, Coram shares his subject's disdain for source notes, giving us no clue as to when and in what context Boyd said this, if he did.

him, the researcher can check the original. But when Boyd simply took notes on his favorite yellow legal pads, the task is daunting. It's not just the occasional reference to Marx and Lenin: the student of Boyd has to live with the possibility that *any* quotation might have been differently emphasized in the original, or even differently phrased. As noted earlier, one of the minds visited by Boyd was that of Thomas Kuhn, who argued that each scientific paradigm brings with it a "set of rules for normal research." Scientists conform to those rules until a crisis shakes their faith and a paradigm shift occurs.[98] Boyd never did conform to the social studies paradigm in the way he studied and wrote, which goes far to explain his low esteem in American universities.

He did keep successive drafts of his briefings—often identifying them as Warp 1, Warp 2, and so on, in tribute to his children's fascination with the television drama *Star Trek*—so we can follow the evolution of his thought. Thus, in the *New Conception (Fast Transients)* brief of 1976, he provides three examples of high-tempo military operations. By the time *Patterns of Conflict* is more or less finalized at the end of 1986, Boyd has assembled a virtual history of warfare from ancient Greece to modern Europe. He finds one common element among the most successful operations: *infiltration tactics*, practiced alike by the Mongol hordes of 1220 and the German storm troopers of 1918. He defines it in a typically dense passage:

> Infiltration fire and movement schemes can be viewed as Napoleon's multi-thrust *strategic* penetration maneuvers being transformed into multi-thrust *tactical* penetration maneuvers down to the lowest operational / organizational level—the squad.[99]

In his early, successful campaigns, Napoleon bewildered his enemies by his flexible use of sharpshooters, horse-drawn artillery, cavalry, and infantry columns. Boyd sees the German squad leader of 1918 as Napoleon writ small, doing on the tactical level what the great Bonaparte had done strategically. (Later, however, Napoleon came to favor centralized command,

---

[98] Kuhn 1962, p. 84.
[99] Boyd 1986, *Patterns of Conflict*, slide 62 (emphasis added).

massed artillery, and a battering-ram approach—high diddle diddle, straight up the middle.)

Applying his tool of deconstruction and reconstruction, Boyd also concludes that the storm troopers, breaking through Allied weak points and attacking targets of opportunity, were operating much like T. E. Lawrence and his Arab cavalry, harassing the Turks in the Middle East: "Both stress clouded / distorted signatures, mobility and cohesion of small units as basis to insert an amorphous yet focused effort into or thru adversary weaknesses."[100]

The excerpts above come from the widely distributed version of *Patterns of Conflict* that Boyd completed in December 1986. As noted, however, he continually refined his briefings. In a version that seems to date from 1995 or 1996, and therefore presumably his final word on the subject, he more closely examines the relationship between blitzkrieg and guerrilla tactics:

<u>Infiltration</u>

• Blitz and guerrillas infiltrate a nation or regime at all levels to soften and shatter the moral fiber of the political, economic and social structure. To carry out this program, a la Sun Tzu, Blitz and Guerrillas:

• Probe and test adversary to unmask strengths, weaknesses, maneuvers, and intentions.

• Shape adversary's perception of the world to manipulate or undermine his plans and actions.

<u>Purpose</u>

• To force capitulations when combined with external political, economic, and military pressures.

or

• To minimize the resistance of a weakened foe for the military blows that will follow.[101]

Boyd doesn't use our favored term—*insurgency*—and in fact there's an argument to be made that it is inadequate to the need.

---

[100] Ibid, slide 65.
[101] Boyd Papers, Box 28, folder 10.

T. E. Lawrence ran a commando campaign against the Turks, as did Paul von Lettow-Vorbeck against the British and South Africans in the same time period, while their home governments fought a conventional war in France and Turkey. Neither man was an insurgent against an established government. (Much the same could be said of Frank Merrill's "Marauders" and Orde Wingate's "Chindits," operating behind Japanese lines in Burma in 1943-1944.) Employing the 19th Century term, Boyd singles out twelve successful guerrilla campaigns:

- American colonists against the British, 1775-1781
- Spanish *guerrillas* against the French in support of the British Army, 1808-1814
- Russian partisans harassing Napoleon's army, 1812
- Paul von Lettow-Vorbeck's forces against the British in German East Africa, 1914-1918
- T. E. Lawrence and the Arab Legion against the Turkish army, 1916-1918
- Chinese Communists against the Nationalist government, 1927-1949, and their parallel war against the Japanese, 1937-1945
- Russian partisans against the Germans, 1941-1945
- Yugoslav partisans against the Germans, 1941-1945
- The Viet Minh against the French, 1945-1954
- Algerian nationalists against the French, 1954-1962
- The Cuban revolution, 1956-1959
- The Viet Cong and the North Vietnamese against the Americans and South Vietnamese, 1958-1975[102]

Similarly, Boyd cites five campaigns in which the guerrillas were unable to achieve their goals:

---

[102] Boyd 1986, *Patterns of Conflict*, slide 97. The lists didn't change in later versions of the briefing.

- Filipinos against the Americans, 1899-1902
- Boers against the British in South Africa, 1900-1902
- Greek Communists against the government, 1944-1949
- *Hukbalahaps* against the Philippine government, 1946-1954
- Malayan Communists against British Commonwealth forces, 1948-1960[103]

To be sure, Boyd's list of insurgencies is not exhaustive. To take two obvious examples, he nowhere addresses the ordeal of the British Army against Irish irregulars through much of the 20th Century, nor the travail of the Soviet Army in Afghanistan in the 1980s. Whether the United States and its NATO allies are to have a similar unhappy experience in Afghanistan is still an open question.

It's interesting and perhaps a bit ominous that—especially in last hundred years—guerrillas have been more successful when fighting an alien power than when they are rebelling against their own government. Indeed, this is more often true than appears at first glance. In the "Malayan Emergency," as they termed it, the British were foreigners but had the advantage of combating an ethnic Chinese minority, so they could present themselves as supporters of the majority Malayan population and government. As a guerrilla leader, Colonel Lettow-Vorbeck in German East Africa was as alien as his adversaries, but he was fluent in Swahili and treated his African troops with affection and respect.

---

[103] Ibid.

# 4 - Counter-blitz, counter-guerrilla

The aggressor generally finds it easier than the defender to get inside his opponent's OODA Loop. Better to be Heinz Guderian, crossing the Meuse on rubber boats and pontoon bridges in the dark, than Maurice-Gustave Gamelin, desperately trying to reinforce the river's west bank. Eleven French divisions were on the march, with the first scheduled to arrive on May 14. Alas for France, 150 German tanks and a considerable body of infantry crossed during the night of May 13, before the first French reinforcements showed up. As Gamelin conceded after the war:

> It was a remarkable maneuver ... a perfect utilization of circumstances. It showed troops and a command that knew how to maneuver, who were organized to operate quickly—as tanks, aircraft, and wireless permitted them to do. It is perhaps the first time that a battle had been won, which became decisive, without having had to engage the bulk of the forces.[104]

But was the French defeat inevitable? Could *Gamelin* somehow have managed to get inside *Guderian's* OODA Loop? Boyd notes that "the amorphous, lethal, and unpredictable" aspects of blitzkrieg attacks "make them appear awesome and unstoppable," thereby producing "uncertainty, doubt, mistrust, confusion, disorder, fear, panic ... and ultimately collapse," much as happens to a pilot losing an air-to-air combat.[105]

Nevertheless, the blitzer faces difficulties of his own. He must keep up the tempo and at the same time maintain the cohesion of his forces, even as he "repeatedly and rapidly" shifts direction, so as to continually pit strength against weakness. Can the defender exploit this vulnerability? Boyd thinks that the

---

[104] Builder et al 1999, who also note that "Up to the breakthrough at Sedan, Guderian executed [his superior's] command concept; thereafter, his concept dominated the operation—even over the opposition of his superiors." Thus, in pushing through to the Channel, Guderian fulfilled his commander's *intent* by going against his *wishes*—a sterling example of Auftragstaktik.

[105] Boyd 1986, *Patterns of Conflict*, slide 101 (ellipses original).

defense can indeed operate in a fashion that mirrors the blitzkrieg, by emphasizing intelligence, air and ground reconnaissance, and a screen of outposts and patrols to give early warning. Behind the forward screen, combined-arms teams (infantry, armor, artillery, and air) should be deployed and constantly re-deployed, to mask their disposition and keep them on a mobile footing. Meanwhile, a mobile armored reserve would stand ready to move quickly "to decapitate any local breakthrough" or to launch a counterstroke. Accepting the same risks as the attacker—i.e., leaving gaps in the defensive line so as to concentrate strength where it is needed—the defender can use ambushes, flank attacks, and thrusts into the enemy rear, in order to "channel as well as drain-away momentum and break-up cohesion of Blitz thrusts."[106]

Just as Heinz Guderian left his flanks exposed in his dash to the Channel, the French commander should have been willing to abandon his fixed defenses in order to move cross-country, attack those open flanks, break the German armored column into multiple columns, and—hopefully—defeat them in detail. As to how this might work in practice, Boyd nowhere says, in large part because (as I shall treat in more detail below) he just didn't believe in institutionalizing solutions to a problem. But Major David Fadok, who in 1994 was writing his master's dissertation at the Air University, suggested two possibilities to Boyd, and both apparently met with his approval:

> For those disappointed readers still looking for an operational example of Boyd's ideas, I offer the following two, both of which were acceptable to Boyd as possible applications. The first ... is the Russian concept of the Operational Maneuver Group ... a combined-arms team of raiders, paratroopers, and diversionary units designed to operate *within* enemy formations....
>
> A second example specifically relates to air power and revolves around another Russian concept, that of the "reconnaissance-strike complex" ... [that] weds real-time intelligence ... to long-range strike platforms ... [that] would engage in parallel warfare against strategic command, control, communications, computer,

---

[106] Boyd 1986, *Patterns of Conflict*, slides 104, 105.

and intelligence ... targets to get inside and disintegrate the enemy's "moral-mental-physical being."[107]

Boyd is suggesting something more than tactics, and more than the operational art described in Major Fadok's examples. "A strategist," wrote one of his favorite authors, Basil Liddell Hart, "should think in terms of paralysing, not of killing.... [A] man killed is merely one man less, whereas a man unnerved is ... capable of spreading an epidemic of panic. On a higher plane ... psychological pressure on the government of a country may suffice to cancel all the resources at its command—so that the sword drops from a paralysed hand."[108]

To revert to the offense, there's an interesting prefiguring here of "Shock and Awe"—the term widely used in the media during the run-up to the U.S. invasion of Iraq in 2003. It was generally, and mistakenly, understood to refer to the aerial bombardment that preceded the actual invasion. In truth, the entire operation, like that of the German invasion of France in 1940, was an example of shock and awe, and the "disorder, fear, panic" such an assault can inflict upon the defender. When the Iraqis did not collapse under the aerial bombardment, television commentators spoke as though the American plan had miscarried. But what if the misinterpretation had been fed to them as a psychological warfare feint, much like the threatened but never materialized Marine landing in the 1991 Gulf War? *Create disorder in their ranks, and take them.... Attack where they are unprepared. Go forth where they will not expect it.*

## Defeating a guerrilla campaign

Boyd then segues into the problem of how to combat an insurgency—indeed, in *Patterns of Conflict*, he treats counter-guerrilla operations under the same heading as counter-blitz. He argues that blitzers and guerrillas both use infiltration tactics to

---

[107] Fadok 1995, p. 21. General Fadok is now Director of Policy and Strategy for the U.S. Southern Command.
[108] Liddle Hart 1954, p. 212.

confuse and defeat their adversaries, and that they in turn can be defeated by applying their own tactics against them.

Fortunately for those who would reconstruct his thinking, Boyd by 1986 has strayed far from the U.S. military model of a briefing slide. A single slide about waging a counter-guerrilla campaign runs to 300 words ... plus a footnote. The object of such a campaign, he begins, is to "Undermine guerrilla cause and destroy their cohesion by demonstrating integrity and competence of government to represent and serve needs of people—rather than exploit and impoverish them for the benefit of a greedy elite." And the footnote: "*If you cannot realize such a political program, you might consider changing sides!*"[109]

It's hard to avoid the suspicion that, in developing this thought over successive versions of the brief, Boyd is thinking of the Saigon regimes to which the U.S. was shackled during the Vietnam War. And likewise with the solutions he offers: as counter-guerrilla, he says, we should "root out and visibly punish corruption." Next we provide "new leaders with recognized competence as well as popular appeal." Finally, we must "Ensure that they deliver justice, eliminate grievances and connect government with grass roots." All very true, of course, and excellent advice for Spanish authorities in their struggle against Basque separatists, but scant guidance for American troops patrolling Helmand province, if only because the Afghan leaders are not ours to provide. Marginally more useful is Boyd's advice that we should infiltrate the guerrilla movement, employ locals for intelligence gathering, and "Seal-off guerrilla regions ... by diplomatic, psychological, and ... other activities that strip-away potential allies as well as by disrupting or straddling communications that connect these regions with outside world."[110]

Alas, it is precisely those insurgencies with access to a safe haven that are most difficult to root out. In the 1960s, the U.S. found it impossible to seal off South Vietnam from infiltration through Laos, Cambodia, and the South China Sea. Even with

---

[109] Boyd 1986, *Patterns of Conflict*, slide 108 (emphasis added).
[110] Ibid.

help from the Pakistani military, American and NATO troops face much the same problem in Afghanistan.

Boyd seems to take the law enforcement rather than the military approach to counterinsurgency: "Deploy administrative talent, police, and counter-guerrilla teams into affected localities," he says, so that we can "inhibit guerrilla ... movement; minimize guerrilla contact with local inhabitants; isolate their ruling cadres; and destroy their infrastructure."[111] Only that last verb—*destroy*— reminds us of the U.S. military that stormed into Iraq in March 2003. And there is some evidence that Boyd has changed his thinking over the years. In an earlier variant of this same slide, the next point begins with the words: "*Take and keep initiative by relentless pursuit.*"[112] No longer: by the time of the published brief, Boyd has abandoned the hot chase and advises us instead to use the presence of the outside teams to build up local governance and recruit local militias, "in order to protect people from the persuasion and coercion efforts of the guerrilla cadres and their fighting units." Only then does he suggest military action:

> Use special teams in a complementary effort to penetrate guerrilla controlled regions. Employ (guerrillas' own) tactics of reconnaissance, infiltration, surprise hit-and-run, and sudden ambush to: keep roving bands off-balance, make base areas untenable, and disrupt communication with the outside world.[113]

Alas, Boyd nowhere defines these "special teams." However, he's probably thinking of something along the lines of the Special Forces troops and Central Intelligence Agency operatives who played a major role in overthrowing the Taliban in the fall of 2001. Whatever their makeup, the teams are to expand from one affected area to another, as advocated by Hubert Lyautey at the end of the 19th Century. The French military had little success with the *tache d'huile* (oil spot) approach in Vietnam in the 1950s, but fared somewhat better with General Lyautey's notion in Algeria. (Ten years after the French debacle at Dien Bien Phu,

---

[111] Ibid.
[112] Boyd Papers, Box 16, folder 16 (emphasis added), a version that seems to date from 1984, two years before the published brief.
[113] Boyd 1986, *Patterns of Conflict*, slide 108.

American advisers were following a similar policy in Vietnam. They called it the "oil slick," perhaps a conflation of the French term and the sailor's trick of spreading oil upon troubled waters.) Boyd concludes his counter-guerrilla slide with this final bit of advice:

> Break guerrillas' moral-mental-physical hold over the population, destroy their cohesion, and bring about their collapse via political initiative that demonstrates <u>moral legitimacy</u> and <u>vitality</u> of government and by relentless military operations that emphasize <u>stealth / fast-tempo / fluidity-of-action</u> and <u>cohesion</u> of overall effort.[114]

So Boyd has moved "relentless" to the end of the queue, and he has married it to infiltration techniques.

If this all seems hopelessly vague, two things at least are clear. First, Boyd doesn't like what we now—daintily—know as "kinetic" operations—that is, the application of military force, or what soldiers more honestly call "breaking things and killing people." In May 1989 he received the final draft of a field manual entitled *Military Operations in Low-Intensity Conflict*, which as was his custom he underlined, starred, and annotated with heavy slashes of his ballpoint pen. He double-starred this passage, which could well have come from his own musings on the Orientation phase of the OODA Loop: "The leaders of the insurgency ... must gain popular support. Their key tasks are to break the ties between the people and the government and to establish their own movement's credibility.... *Their education, background, family, social connections, and experiences shape how they think, what they want, and how they will fulfill their goals.*" (This passage appears unchanged in the manual as published the following year.) I don't for a moment believe that the Boydian language is a coincidence: 1989 was about the high point of his influence with the U.S. military.[115]

The field manual assumes, and Boyd clearly agrees, that American counterinsurgency operations 1) will be rare and 2) will

---

[114] Ibid.
[115] Boyd Papers, Box 12, folder 7 (emphasis added); U.S. Army 1990, Ch. 2, p. 2.

be conducted in concert with an existing local government—as opposed to overturning that government, as we did in Afghanistan in October 2001 and Iraq in April 2003. He heavily underlines, stars, and crosses out one revealing word in this sentence: *"Destruction of the infrastructure and elimination of the conditions which cause the insurgency must be the domain of the host nation* ~~armed~~ *forces."* Alas, the deletion wasn't accepted, and the published manual retains the primacy of *armed* forces.[116]

Also clear, I think, is that while Boyd was perfectly willing to *annotate* a field manual, he would never himself have caused one to be written. The absence of specificity in his writings isn't the result of fuzzy thinking or of a puckish pleasure in being obscure—almost certainly it's a deliberate choice. Boyd believes in policy but not in doctrine. Or at any rate he doesn't believe in articulating a single doctrine, such as the recent and much applauded *Counterinsurgency Field Manual*, precisely tailored to the requirements of Iraq, but seemingly unable to gain much traction in Afghanistan.[117] "We have doctrine," Boyd cautioned his audience at the Air War College in 1992, in the question period following his *Conceptual Spiral* briefing:

> The Air Force has got a doctrine, the Army's got a doctrine, Navy's got a doctrine, everybody's got a doctrine. [But if you] read my work, "doctrine" doesn't appear in there even once. You can't find it. You know why I don't have it in there? Because it's doctrine on day one, and every day after it becomes dogma. That's why....

> Well, I understand you're going to have to write doctrine, and that's all right... [But] even after you write it, assume it's not right. And look at a whole lot of other doctrines—German doctrine, other kinds of doctrines—and learn those too. And then you've got a bunch of doctrines, and the reason you want to learn them all [is so that] you're not captured by any one, and you can lift stuff out

---

[116] Boyd Papers, Box 12, folder 7 (emphasis added); U.S. Army 1990, Ch. 2, p. 46.
[117] U.S. Army 2007.

of here, stuff out of there.... You can put your snowmobile [together], and you do better than anyone else.

If you got one doctrine, you're a dinosaur. Period.[118]

As Antoine Bousquet summarizes John Boyd's thinking in *The Scientific Way of Warfare*, "Boyd believes in a perpetually renewed world that is 'uncertain, ever-changing, unpredictable' and thus requires continually revising, adapting, destroying and recreating our theories and systems to deal with it." Grant Hammond expresses it this way: "*Ambiguity* is central to Boyd's vision ... not something to be feared but something that is a given.... We never have complete and perfect information. We are never completely sure of the consequences of our actions.... The best way to succeed ... is to revel in ambiguity."[119]

For Boyd, counterinsurgency—*all* war, *all* competition, and indeed all human activity—can be viewed as an extended and fatal game of Parkour, the extreme sport in which practitioners take the physical world on the run, trusting to their muscle, skill, and reflexes to flow over the obstacles the world puts in their path. Parkour, unlike football and other organized sports, has no rules ... and neither does life. A generation before Boyd, the admirable scholar-journalist Bernard Fall made a similar point with respect to the then-burgeoning American effort in South Vietnam: "I would like to close," he wrote, "with one last thought, which applies, of course, to everything that is done in the armed forces, but particularly to revolutionary war: *If it works, it is obsolete.*"[120] Yesterday's rules won't work today.

That was in 1965. We didn't heed Fall's maxim then, and in 2010 we still seem to be ignoring it. A doctrine President Bush forged in Iraq is obsolete by the time President Obama attempts to apply it to Afghanistan.

---

[118] Boyd 1992d, *Conceptual Spiral* video (the punctuation and paragraphing are mine). The YouTube video of his riff can be seen online at www.youtube.com/watch?v=heWpHSOMAmY [accessed 2 August 2009].
[119] Bousquet 2009, p. 193 (quoting Boyd 1992b, *Conceptual Spiral*, slide 30); Hammond 1997.
[120] Fall 1965.

# The name of the game

Such was the crux of Boyd's counter-guerrilla thought, as expressed in what would be the published version of *Patterns of Conflict*, which he signed with a flourish in December 1986. (There are later versions of the briefing in his papers, but for the most part the language is identical.) However, he was at the same time finalizing another brief, the *Organic Design for Command and Control*, which he had been working on at least since 1982. In essence, this is Boyd's argument that, as he once told a journalist looking for a hook for her story, *"People not weapons win wars."*[121] Command and Control (which the military abbreviates as C&C) shouldn't be a matter of orders sent from the top down, he says, but of information flowing from the bottom up. In this way, the soldier on patrol will serve as the commanding general's eyes—as the Observation phase of the general's OODA Loop. Boyd begins by defining this process as "leadership with monitoring," but he apparently decides that this formulation is too rigid, for he quickly refines it to "appreciation and leadership."[122] Far from commanding and controlling, the general should be guiding the troops. Like so many of Boyd's ideas, this one was born in the German army and is now the conventional wisdom—at least on paper—in most western armed forces.

The C&C brief was accompanied by the even more mystically titled *The Strategic Game of ? and ?*. The briefing doesn't explicitly address counter-insurgency, but it does provide clues to how Boyd might have developed a counter-insurgency doctrine—or perhaps I should say "anti-doctrine." It contains an instructive four-slide section titled "Name-of-the-Game," which in an early version begins with the standard Boydian premise: *'Be adaptable and unpredictable so that adversary can neither ascertain nor anticipate our moves."*[123] (I have posted a copy of the draft slide at www.danford.net/boyd/name.htm.) Inevitably, as

---

[121] Amidon 1981.
[122] Boyd 1987a, *Organic Design*, slide 32. For a more elaborate discussion, see Osinga 2007, pp. 189-200.
[123] Boyd Papers, Box 16, folder 4 (emphasis added). This handwritten draft probably dates to 1982.

he massages his phrasing over the years and after many oral presentations, that simple statement morphs into something almost too complex to be understood at first reading:

<u>NAME-OF-THE-GAME</u>

- Use moral leverage to amplify our spirit and strength as well as expose the flaws of competing or adversary systems, all the while influencing the uncommitted, potential adversaries and current adversaries so that they are drawn toward our philosophy and empathetic toward our success;

or put another way

- Preserve or build-up our moral authority while compromising that of our adversaries' in order to pump-up our resolve, drain-away adversaries' resolve, and attract them as well as others to our cause and way of life.[124]

The name of the game, therefore, is *moral leverage*, and that term becomes the heading for the following three slides. Boyd of course doesn't limit "the game" to countering insurgencies, but that's my particular interest, and his advice is wonderfully appropriate.

**Ourselves.** First we must identify our own "blemishes, flaws, or contradictions" and find ways to overcome them. These negative qualities, Boyd warns, alienate us from one another and "thereby destroy our internal harmony, paralyze us, and make it difficult [for us] to cope with an uncertain, everchanging world." At the same time, in true OODA Loop fashion, we should emphasize those "cultural traditions, previous experiences, and unfolding events" that are likely to build up our own harmony and trust, both as individuals and as a society.[125]

**Our adversaries.** At the same time, Boyd continues, we must examine our adversaries' beliefs about "our culture, our achievements, our fitness to exist"—not so much to rebut those beliefs as to remind ourselves that "our survival and place in the

---

[124] Boyd 1987b, *Strategic Game*, slide 54. The question marks in the title stand for *Interaction* and *Isolation* (slide 33). Again, the publication date is deceptive: Boyd worked on these briefs for years. For a synopsis, see Osinga 2007, pp. 201-218.
[125] Ibid, slide 55.

scheme of things is not necessarily a birthright, but is always at risk." Having examined our own "mismatches," as he terms them, we can examine the flaws of the other side, demonstrating to our adversaries—and to the world—that they are inept, corrupt, and unsavory. Finally, we acquaint them with "our philosophy and way of life" so as to demonstrate that their behavior violates "the dignity and the needs of the individual [and] the security and well-being of society as a whole."[126] This may sound a bit like the tub-thumping jingoism of an earlier day, but recall that Boyd wants us to look at our blemishes first, and only then to point out the spots on Osama bin Laden's face.

**All the rest.** Finally, having sorted our own situation and that of our opponents, we should turn to "the uncommitted or potential adversaries"—the rest of the world, in short. In this regard, we must:

- Respect their culture and achievements, show them we bear them no harm, and help them adjust to an unfolding world, as well as provide additional benefits and more favorable treatment for those who support our philosophy and way of doing things;

yet

- Demonstrate that we neither tolerate nor support those ideas and interactions that undermine ... our culture and our philosophy hence our interests and our fitness to cope with a changing world.[127]

This book began, remember, as a thesis in the War Studies department of King's College London. When I first outlined Boyd's ideas for my thesis adviser, he commented that they are "not a million miles from what [counter-insurgency] theorists such as Thompson, Kitson, [and] Galula said."[128] True enough: even before the Vietnam War escalated beyond the American ability to contain it, David Galula warned: "On the eve of embarking on a major effort, the counterinsurgent faces what is probably the most difficult problem of the war: *He has to arm himself with a competing cause*." Yet I find no evidence that Boyd ever read Galula or the other practitioner-theorists of counterinsurgency.

---
[126] Ibid, slide 56.
[127] Ibid, slide 57.
[128] Betz 2009.

Their books are not among the hundreds cited in his copious notes, nor are they included in his library now shelved at the Gray Research Center at Quantico, Virgina.[129]

## On being in the village

Not long after finalizing the *Strategic Game*, Boyd had occasion to view Oliver Stone's feature film about the Vietnam War. *Platoon* won the "best film" Academy Award in May 1987 and was afterward released as a video recording. This was probably when Boyd saw it, for he first mentions the film in notes for a speech he delivered to "USAF officers" in February 1988.[130]

*Platoon* hinges on a combat patrol by the eponymous U.S. Army unit "somewhere near the Cambodian border" toward the end of the Vietnam War. A soldier disappears overnight, and his comrades find his mutilated body in the morning. Soon after, they enter a village with the usual population of old men, women, and children—and the usual overabundance of rice—seeming proof that it is a Viet Cong base, with the young men either hiding in the rain forest or off on a combat mission of their own. The Americans don't speak Vietnamese; the villagers don't speak English. Misunderstandings arise, tension becomes rage, and an American clubs a youngster to death. Others begin shooting, and there's an attempted rape. Though supposedly based on the director's own experiences in South Vietnam, the film clearly owes as much or more to the 1968 massacre at My Lai 4, like most Vietnam War films released in the 1980s. And indeed, My Lai was atypical only because of the scale of the atrocity: "Throughout Vietnam," in the words of Francis (Bing) West, who was himself a Marine officer in that conflict, "there were instances of Americans killing in the hamlets, driven by anger or fear, terrified and ignorant, believing every villager was a Viet Cong."[131]

---

[129] Galula 2006b, p. 71 (emphasis added). For Dr. Betz's other examples, see Frank Kitson, *Low Intensity Operations,* and Robert Thompson, *Revolutionary War in World Strategy, 1945-1969.*
[130] Boyd Papers, Box 16, folder 7.
[131] West 2002, p. 356.

In his scrawled notes for his presentation, Boyd first cites "G—H—2nd Law," for his customary trinity of Gödel's Proof, Heisenberg's Uncertainty Principle, and the Second Law of Thermodynamics. He then segues (and no doubt the shift was a great relief to the Air Force officers) into a discussion of the "25-year war" in Vietnam. "What have I learned since then?" he rhetorically asks. And in the next line he answers: "Terrain doesn't wage war ... people do and with their minds." And in the line after that he writes: "impression (movie *Platoon*)."[132] As one of his listeners remembers the presentation, Boyd described the movie's portrayal of troops going berserk. He concluded by telling the officers: *"We should be the ones in the village, not the people attacking the village."*[133]

That's the point I want to make, but since I began by quoting Boyd's notes, I may as well continue. Boyd goes on to write:

- So what are we good at – ? – (logistics / technology).
- In other words [we] try to bury them with our technology and logistics system.
- Point: Our image of our[selves?] is hardware.[134]

In short: *People not weapons win wars!*

That being the case, it's a pity that Boyd never seems to have read Bing West's memoir of a very different encounter between Americans and Vietnamese. First published in 1972, at a time when few Americans were willing to read a book or watch a film about the conflict, *The Village* is in my opinion a classic of the Vietnam War. It tells the story of the Combined Action Platoon assigned to Binh Nghia, a village of 5,000 souls living in seven settlements near the South China Sea in Quang Nai province. "To the men of the 1st Marine Division who were stationed in the district," West writes, "Binh Nghia was just another village, with nothing peculiar to mark it. If the Marines approached on a large-unit sweep, they would find no traces of the enemy. If they happened to pass through one of its hamlets

---

[132] Boyd Papers, Box 16, folder 7.
[133] Wilson 2005, slide 7. The wording is confirmed by Chet Richards, though he dates the briefing in the following year (Richards 2009).
[134] Boyd Papers, Box 16, folder 7.

on a small patrol, they would likely receive some harassing fire from distant treelines. The villagers were uncommunicative, but not sullen."[135]

To judge by my own experience as a reporter in South Vietnam, this is a spot-on description of American-Vietnamese interaction almost anywhere in the countryside in the 1960s. For Binh Nghia, however, the equation changed when a dozen U.S. Marines took up residence there in June 1966, to defend it on an ongoing basis with the help of triple their number of Vietnamese. The indigenous forces were about equally divided between national police and "Popular Force" militiamen, whom the Americans called Puffs. With varying success and numerous casualties—nine Marines died during the two years they were stationed in Binh Nghia, along with a larger number of police and Puffs—the Combined Action Platoon stabilized the community so well that the Americans could be withdrawn.

Bing West revisited Binh Nghia as a civilian in 1971, by which time the war had moved elsewhere and a single militia platoon sufficed to keep order. "The village is intact," he wrote in an epilogue to his book. "The village has endured." He returned again in 2001, to find Binh Nghia doubled in size and bearing a new name, courtesy of the regime in Hanoi: Binh Chuc, meaning "Just Peace." Yet the Marines of the Combined Action Platoon were so fondly remembered that a shrine and communal well, built by them and the local people in 1967, still bore an inscription in the Americans' honor. "The village remembers," West wrote then.[136]

And what is most extraordinary about all this is that Binh Nghia is only four miles distant from the massacre site at My Lai 4. John Boyd would have loved the symmetry.

---

[135] West 2002, p. 12. A Combined Action Platoon would ordinarily be commanded by a sergeant, but Captain West was given the job so he could write an assessment of the program.
[136] Ibid, pp. 14-15, 347, 349.

# The War on Terror

Alas, the Marines' success with the Combined Action Platoons was not replicated by the U.S. Army, during the Vietnam War or after, with consequences that became painfully evident during its occupation of Iraq. That's an irony, for John Boyd more than any other individual provided the intellectual foundation of the U.S. military that so successfully stormed through Iraq in the spring of 2003 . . . which is not to say that he would have approved of the invasion, or indeed of the way the United States conducted its "Global War on Terror" following the al-Qaeda attacks of September 2001. *People not weapons win wars!*

Interestingly, the situation in Iraq began to turn around for the U.S. military in the so-called "surge," when among other innovations it turned to something like the Vietnam-era Combined Action Platoon. The journalist Tom Ricks—no great admirer of George W. Bush's Iraq adventure—wrote about the surge in a book tellingly entitled *The Gamble*. He cites the battle of Tarmiyah in February 2007, when al-Qaeda in Iraq (AQI) ran the Iraqi police out of the town north of Baghdad, as they had done in so many other communities. This time, however, thirty-eight Americans of the 1st Cavalry Division moved into the abandoned police station. AQI tried to run them out, too, assaulting the station one morning with rifle fire, rockets, and a monster truck bomb. "The battle that followed," Ricks tells us, "resembled the movie *Zulu*, in which a small detachment of British soldiers fends off thousands of African warriors." One soldier died, twenty-eight were wounded, and the police station was destroyed—but not overrun. By sundown the 1st Cav had set up a new base in an abandoned schoolhouse nearby. No longer would U.S. soldiers "commute to war," in the formulation that became popular in Baghdad and Washington during the surge. Increasingly, as 2007 wore on, the Americans became the people in the village.[137]

Boyd would have applauded the change in strategy, though I suspect he would have wondered why the 1st Cav troopers

---

[137] Ricks 2009, pp. 166, 181-85. The casualty count is not consistent.

didn't follow the Marines' prescription of tripling their number with indigenous forces. Absent the local police and militiamen, the Marines would have found it difficult, if not impossible, to secure Binh Nghia in 1967. As David Galula writes of his years as a company commander in France's attempt to hold on to its Algerian colony: "They were Moslems and we were not. The rebel fish could swim better in Moslem water than the counterinsurgent land mammal. The more reason for us to rely on Moslem supporters."[138]

Could such a policy work in Afghanistan? The task would be daunting, to say the least: David Kilcullen tells us that the country has no fewer than 40,020 villages.[139] To put a Combined Action Platoon in each, following the Binh Nghia formula, would require 480,000 foreign troops and 1,440,000 Afghans, or several orders of magnitude greater than the available forces. Obviously something less than blanket coverage would have to suffice—and might very well do so. As Bernard Fall proposed for countering the Viet Cong, *quadrillage* rather than *tache d'huile* may be the better strategy—that is, not oil spots but "griddage."

"One doesn't start from the center of something and work one's way out," Fall explained, "but he starts from the periphery and works one's way *in*."[140] His reversal of the conventional wisdom is, I think, something John Boyd would have found congenial. *If it works, it is obsolete!* (And indeed, something like quadrillage seemed to underlie General Stanley McChrystal's offensive in Afghanistan in the late winter of 2010.)

Yet all this begs the question of whether a military approach is ever the desirable one. Boyd's acolytes mostly take a dim view of the American interventions in Iraq and Afghanistan. Chet Richards, for example, has argued that it would be worthwhile actually to dismantle much of the U.S. military, "eliminating active Army armor and mechanized infantry divisions" in favor of the

---

[138] Galula 2006a, p. 70.
[139] Kilcullen 2009, p. 47.
[140] Fall 1965. The more closely I read this essay, the more prescient it seems: its first section is titled "The Century of 'Small Wars'." Fall was writing ten years before the last American helicopter lifted off from the U.S. embassy in Saigon.

lean and mobile U.S. Marines, backed by the Army Reserve.[141] The conservative thinker Bill Lind, who helped formalize Boyd's theories into the concept of fourth-generation warfare, is a caustic critic of our military operations in Afghanistan, and especially our use of remotely piloted drone aircraft. "To themselves and onlookers," Lind writes, the Taliban and al-Qaeda "are David and the U.S. is Goliath. In the 3,000 or so years that the biblical story has been told, how many listeners have identified with the giant?"[142]

Boyd himself is lyrical in his plea for a strategy that is more spiritual and less kinetic:

[F]or success over the long haul and under the most difficult conditions, one needs some unifying vision that can be used to attract the uncommitted as well as pump-up friendly resolve and drive and drain-away or subvert adversary resolve and drive ... *a vision rooted in human nature so noble, so attractive that it not only attracts the uncommitted and magnifies the spirit and strength of its adherents, but also undermines the dedication and determination of any competitors or adversaries....* A grand ideal, overarching theme, or noble philosophy ... within which individuals as well as societies can shape and adapt to unfolding circumstances—yet offers a way to expose flaws of competing or adversary systems.[143]

Even the most devoted admirer of President Bush would be hard put to argue that he offered "a grand ideal" or "noble philosophy" to justify the American invasions of Afghanistan and Iraq. Regime change hardly qualifies, nor does eradicating weapons of mass destruction—nor even the hope of bringing Osama bin Laden to justice. Mr. Bush did better with his proclaimed goal of promoting democracy in Muslim lands, but it was clearly grafted onto a policy adopted for more immediate

---

[141] Richards 2003, p. 64.
[142] Lind 2009, "Droning On." For an amusing and informative expansion of this thought, see the mock field manual, Lind et al 2009.
[143] Boyd 1986, *Patterns of Conflict*, slides 143-44 (emphasis added). As an example of how Boyd's thinking has spread to the business world, the "grand ideal" sentence is quoted in full in a study of how American corporations can cope with the "Sarbox" restrictions mentioned earlier (Quartermain 2006, p. 86).

reasons. The famously eloquent Barack Obama may succeed better at counteracting the Taliban and like-minded jidhadists, but (at least during his first year) he seems content merely to change his predecessor's vocabulary, rather than his strategy, which can best be summarized as reinforce-and-persist.

If Mr. Obama finds himself unable to articulate that grand ideal—that noble philosophy—then perhaps it will be time to retreat to John Boyd's fallback position, as advanced in his sly footnote to *Patterns of Conflict*: "If you cannot realize such a political program, you might consider changing sides!"

## Conclusion

For three centuries, Western thought was grounded in the mechanistic world-view bequeathed to us by Isaac Newton and René Descartes. Change was slow in coming, with the first stirrings from the existentialist philosophers toward the end of the 19th Century. "God is dead," as Friedrich Nietzsche famously declared—or He wasn't, in the equally tormented view of Søren Kierkegaard. In the 20th Century, the baton was passed from the existentialists to creative artists like James Joyce and Pablo Picasso, then to scientific thinkers like Albert Einstein, Werner Heisenberg, and Kurt Gödel, and then again to literary scholars like Jacques Derrida. Finally it reached the military in the person of John Boyd, whom it is not too farfetched to describe as our first "postmodern" strategist. Unlike those who fought the great attritional wars of the past 200 years—titanic clashes between populations organised for war—we cannot fall back on familiar certainties. Rather, we have our boots firmly planted in flux. "It was as if the ground had been pulled out from under one," as Einstein himself expressed it, "with no firm foundation anywhere, upon which one could have built."[144] The uncertainty principle has by now permeated philosophy, the arts, science, the social sciences, the humanities and—perhaps certainty's last bastion—military strategy.

---

[144] Quoted in Kuhn 1962, p. 83.

One of uncertainty's mileposts was the April 2003 dash to Baghdad by the 3rd Infantry Division and 1st Marine Division, arguably one of the great military operations of all time. Whatever followed from George Bush's adventure in Iraq, the "March Up" at least was a success, and John Boyd's briefing slides did as much as anything to make it possible.

John Boyd began by providing a conceptual framework for the now almost obsolete challenge of air-to-air combat. (Not in this century has a fighter pilot of any nationality shot down an enemy aircraft. The most recent such victor appears to have been Lt. Col. Michael Geczy USAF, credited with downing a Yugoslav MiG-29 on June 4, 1999. He was flying the F-15C Eagle that Boyd helped nurture.) Boyd expanded the OODA Loop first to warfare generally, then to any contest between individuals or groups, and finally to the problem of human survival in an ever-changing universe.

At the same time, he deepened it to include the parallel endeavors of the scientist or engineer—and perhaps indeed those of the student of War in the Modern World—progressing from observation to orientation to hypothesis to test. Thus, I *observe* a threat in the person of Osama bin Laden, Ayman al-Zawahiri, and their associates. I *orient* myself to that threat, bringing to the table my enlisted service in the U.S. Army, my months as a reporter in South Vietnam, my cultural and ideological predispositions, my three years in the War Studies program at King's College London, and a trove of new information from the Boyd canon. I *hypothesize* that the Combined Action Platoon of the Vietnam War might have provided a useful tool for pacifying Iraq and Afghanistan. Then I *test* my hypothesis against the reality of 40,020 Afghan villages, and find that I must return to the drawing board. Thus I cycle through a student's version of the fighter pilot's OODA Loop, or OOHT Loop, if you prefer. In any event, better luck next time!

The process has no end. We cannot hope to stop change, as John Boyd tells us again and again. But perhaps we can learn to thrive in it.

# Bibliography

The "Papers of Colonel John R. Boyd (USAF)" are archived as Collection 2062 at the U.S. Marine Corps Archives and Special Collections, located at the Gray Research Center, Quantico, Virginia. They comprise 31 boxes of notes, briefings, correspondence, press cuttings, and miscellaneous papers (accessed 5-8 May 2009), which I cite as "Boyd Papers" with the box number and a folder number if applicable. There are a further four boxes containing machine copies of extracts from books and periodicals. Unless otherwise credited, the graphics in this book are copies of the originals in the Boyd Papers, Box 25.

The comprehensive "brief," titled *A Discourse on Winning and Losing* (see Boyd 1992a below), was widely distributed in a spiral-bound edition. Boyd called it "the Green Book" after its cover, but the version on file at the Gray Research Center has a blue cover. Though dated August 1987, it was almost certainly printed five years later, since it includes the *Conceptual Spiral*, which Boyd finished in July/August 1992. If referencing a briefing as it appears in the Green Book, I cite it by the date Boyd wrote on its opening page; if an earlier or later version, I cite the appropriate folder in the Boyd Papers. I have posted the scanned individual briefs of the *Discourse* online.

You can approximate a Boyd briefing by listening to the audio of his *Conceptual Spiral* presentation to the USAF Air War College (cited below as Boyd 1992b) while viewing the actual briefing slides online (Boyd 1992c), and following that with the video of the question-and-answer session at the same presentation (Boyd 1992d).

Amidon, Mary (1981), "Boyd's Philosophy: 'People Not Weapons Win Wars'," in Eire PA *Times-News*, p. 13-A, 20 September 1981.

Balck, Hermann (1979), "Translation of Taped Conversation with General Hermann Balck, 13 April 1979" (Columbus OH: Battelle Columbus Laboratories). Online: www.dtic.mil/cgi-bin/GetTRDoc?AD=ADA160511&Location= U2&doc=GetTRDoc.pdf [accessed 21 July 2009].

Berkowitz, Bruce (2003), "John Boyd: The American Sun Tzu," in *Orbis*, Vol. 47, No. 2, pp. 370-375.

Betz, David (2009), "COIN and OODA," email to the author, 23 September 2009.

Bin Laden, Osama (1996), "Declaration of War against the Americans Occupying the Land of the Two Holy Places," in *Al Quds Al Arabi*, August 1996. Online: www.pbs.org/newshour/terrorism/international/fatwa_1996.html [accessed 13 August 2009].

Bousquet, Antoine (2009), *The Scientific Way of Warfare: Order and Chaos on the Battlefields of Modernity* (New York NY: Columbia University Press).

Boyd, John (1964), *Aerial Attack Study* (Nellis Air Force Base NV: Tactical Air Command), revision of the 1960 original. Online: www.danford.net/boyd/aerialattack.pdf [accessed 28 March 2010].

Boyd, John (1976a), *Destruction and Creation* monograph, in the *Discourse* below. Online: www.danford.net/boyd/destruction.htm [accessed 28 March 2010].

Boyd, John (1976b), *New Conception for Air-to-Air Combat* (*Fast Transients*) briefing. Boyd Papers, Box 3, folder 11. Online: www.danford.net/boyd//fast_transients.pdf [accessed 28 March 2010].

Boyd, John (1977), transcript of USAF oral history interview by John Dick, 28 January1977, at Albert Simpson Historical Research Center, Maxwell Air Force Base AL, with Boyd's handwritten corrections (Boyd Papers, Box 24, folder 10).

Boyd, John (1986), *Patterns of Conflict* briefing, in the *Discourse* below. Online: www.danford.net/boyd/patterns.pdf [accessed 28 March 2010].

Boyd, John (1987a), *Organic Design for Command and Control* briefing, in the *Discourse* below. Online: www.danford.net/boyd/organic.pdf [accessed 28 March 2010].

Boyd, John (1987b), *Strategic Game of ? and ?* briefing, in the *Discourse* below. Online: www.danford.net/boyd/strategic.pdf [accessed 28 March 2010].

Boyd, John (1992a), *A Discourse on Winning and Losing* (also known as "the Green Book"; dated 1987; privately printed), comprising the *Conceptual Spiral, Patterns of Conflict, Organic Design, Strategic Game*, and *Destruction and Creation*, with an introduction and conclusion. Author's collection. The date is my best guess.

Boyd, John (1992b), *Conceptual Spiral* briefing, in the *Discourse* above. Online: www.danford.net/boyd/conceptual.pdf [accessed 28 March 2010].

Boyd, John (1992c), *Conceptual Spiral* briefing (audio, Air War College, Maxwell Air Force Base AL). Online: homepage.mac.com/ace354/Boyd/iMovieTheater38.html [accessed 26 May 2009].

Boyd, John (1992d), *Conceptual Spiral* question and answer session (video, Air War College, Maxwell Air Force Base AL). Online: homepage.mac.com/ace354/Boyd/iMovieTheater39.html [accessed 26 May 2009].

Boyd, John (1996), *The Essence of Winning and Losing* briefing. Online: www.danford.net/boyd/essence.htm [accessed 28 March 2010]. Revision of the 1995 briefing.

Boyer, Peter (2003), "The New War Machine," in *The New Yorker*, 30 June 2003.

Brehmer, Berndt (2005), *The Dynamic OODA Loop: Amalgamating Boyd's OODA Loop and the Cybernetic Approach to Command and Control* (Stockholm: Swedish National Defence College, Department of War Sciences). Online: www.dodccrp.org/events/10th_ICCRTS/CD/papers/365.pdf [accessed 22 November 2008].

Builder, Carl, Steven Bankes, and Richard Nordin (1999), "The Technician: Guderian's Breakthrough at Sedan," in *Command Concepts: A Theory Derived from the Practice of Command and Control* (Santa Monica CA: RAND Corporation). Online: http://www.rand.org/pubs/monograph_reports/2006/MR775.pdf [accessed 26 July 2009].

Bungay, Stephen (2005), "The Road to Mission Command: The Genesis of a Command Philosophy," in *British Army Review*, No. 137. Collection of Eitan Shamir.

Campbell, Douglas (2003), *The Warthog and the Close Air Support Debate* (Annapolis MD: Naval Institute Press).

Clausewitz, Carl von (1976), *On War*, edited and translated by Michael Howard and Peter Paret (Princeton NJ: Princeton University Press).

Coram, Robert (2002), *Boyd: The Fighter Pilot Who Changed the Art of War* (New York NY & Boston MA: Back Bay Books).

Coram, Robert (2003), C-SPAN interview with Brian Lamb. Online: www.booknotes.org/Transcript/?ProgramID=1712 [accessed 15 March 2010].

Fadok, David (1995), *John Boyd and John Warden: Air Power's Quest for Strategic Paralysis* (Maxwell AFB AL: Air University Press).

Fall, Bernard (1965), "The Theory and Practice of Insurgency and Counterinsurgency," in *Naval War College Review*, Vol. 17, No. 8, pp. 21-38.

Fredriksen, John (1999), *Warbirds: An Illustrated Guide to U.S. Military Aircraft, 1915-2000* (Santa Barbara CA: ABC-CLIO).

Freedman, Lawrence (2007), untitled review in *Foreign Affairs*, Vol. 86, No. 5, p.170.

Galula, David (2006a), *Pacification in Algeria, 1956-1958* (Santa Monica CA: RAND Corporation). Reprint of the 1963 edition.

Galula, David (2006b), *Counterinsurgency Warfare: Theory and Practice* (Westport CT: Praeger Security International). Reprint of the 1964 edition.

Gray, Colin (1999), *Modern Strategy* (Oxford: Oxford University Press).

Gray, Colin (2006), *Another Bloody Century: Future War* (London: Phoenix). Reprint of the 2005 edition.

Hammes, Thomas (2005), "War Evolves Into the Fourth Generation," in *Contemporary Security Policy* (Vol. 26, No. 2, pp.189-221).

Hammond, Grant (1997), "The Essential Boyd." Online: www.danford.net/boyd /hammond.htm [accessed 28 March 2010].

Hammond, Grant (2001), *The Mind of War: John Boyd and American Security* (Washington DC: Smithsonian Books).

Keegan, John (1987), *The Mask of Command* (New York NY: Viking).

Kilcullen, David (2009), *The Accidental Guerrilla: Fighting Small Wars in the Midst of a Big One* (New York NY: Oxford University Press USA).

Kuhn, Thomas (1962), *The Structure of Scientific Revolutions* (Chicago IL: University of Chicago Press).

Liddle Hart, Basil (1991), *Strategy* (New York NY: Meridian), reprint of the 1954 2nd revised edition.

Lind, William (1985), *Maneuver Warfare Handbook* (Boulder CO and London: Westview Press).

Lind, William (2009), "Droning On: Remote-controlled mayhem does not win wars," in *The American Conservative*, September 2009. Online: amconmag.com/article/2009/sep/01/00016/ [accessed 14 August 2009].

Lind, William, Keith Nightengale, John Schmitt, Joseph Sutton, and Gary Wilson (1989), "The Changing Face of War: Into the Fourth Generation," in *Marine Corps Gazette*, October 1989. Online: globalguerrillas.typepad.com/lind/the-changing-face-of-war-into-the-fourth-generation.html [accessed 16 April 2010].

Lind, William, and the "Fourth Generation seminar" (2009), *How to Fight in a 4th Generation Insurgency,* "Fleet Marine Force Manual 3-25" (Quantico VA: Expeditionary Warfare School). Online: www.danford.net/boyd/fourth.pdf [accessed 21 November 2009].

Lindberg, Jarmo (2006), "USAF Col John Boyd: From Fighter Tactics to the Art of War." Online: www.sci.fi/~fta/JohnBoyd.htm [accessed 17 May 2009].

Luttwak, Edward (1987), *Strategy: The Logic of War and Peace* (Cambridge MA: Belknap Press, Harvard University Press).

Olds, Robin, with Christina Olds and Ed Rasimus (2010), *Fighter Pilot: The Memoirs of Legendary Ace Robin Olds* (New York NY: St. Martin's Press).

Ortmann, Sven (2009), "About light infantry tactics and the tactical challenges in Afghanistan." Online: www.danford.net/boyd/ortmann.htm [accessed 28 March 2010].

Osinga, Frans (2007), *Science, Strategy and War: The Strategic Theory of John Boyd* (London and New York NY: Routledge).

Osinga, Frans (2009), "F-16," email to the author, 2 June 2009.

Quartermain, John (2006), *Risk Management Solutions for Sarbanes-Oxley Section 404 IT Compliance* (Indianapolis IN: Wiley Publishing).

Ratley, Lonnie III (1977), "A Comparison of the USAF Projected A-10 Employment in Europe and the Luftwaffe Schlachtgeschwader Experience on the Eastern Front in World War Two," MA thesis (Monterey CA: Naval Postgraduate School). Online: www.dtic.mil/cgi-bin/GetTRDoc?AD=ADA036863&Location= U2&doc=GetTRDoc.pdf [accessed 21 July 2009].

Ratley, Lonnie III (2009), "Dissertation," email to the author, 21 July 2009.

Richards, Chester (2003), *A Swift, Elusive Sword: What if Sun Tzu and John Boyd Wrote a National Defense Review?* (Washington DC: Center for Defense Information). Second edition.

Richards, Chester (2004), *Certain to Win* (Bloomington IN: Xlibris).

Richards, Chester (2009), "We Should Be the Villagers," emails to the author, 30 January 2009, 11 August 2009.

Ricks, Thomas (2009), *The Gamble: General David Petraeus and the American Military Adventure in Iraq, 2006-2008* (New York NY: Penguin Press).

Rudel, Hans-Ulrich (1976), "Interview Oberst a.D. Hans-Ulrich Rudel," in Ratley 1997 above, pp. 185-190.

Sageman, Marc (2004), *Understanding Terror Networks* (Philadelphia PA: University of Pennsylvania Press).

Sawyer, Ralph (2007), *The Tao of Deception: Unorthodox Warfare in Historic and Modern China* (New York NY: Basic Books).

Sayen, John (2008), "The Overburden of America's Outdated Defenses," in Winslow Wheeler, editor, *America's Defense Meltdown, Pentagon Reform for President Obama and the New Congress* (Washington DC: Center for Defense Information), pp.1-25.

Spinney, Franklin (1997), "Genghis John," *Proceedings of the U.S. Naval Institute*, Vol. 123, No. 6, pp. 42-47.

Spinney, Franklin (2009), "John Boyd as counter-insurgent," email to the author, 14 July 2009.

Sun-tzu (1994), *The Art of War*, translated by Ralph Sawyer (Boulder CO and Oxford: Westview Press).

U.S. Army (1990), *FM 100-20: Military Operations in Low Intensity Conflict.* Online: www.enlisted.info/field-manuals/fm-100-20-military-operations-in-low-intensity-conflict.shtml [accessed 21 May 2009].

U.S. Army (2007), *FM 3-24: Counterinsurgency Field Manual* (Chicago IL: University of Chicago Press).

Watts, Barry (1995), notes on a telephone conversation with John Boyd, 21 November 1995, in Boyd Papers, Box 28, folder 2.

West, Bing (2002), *The Village* (New York NY: Pocket Books), reprint of the 1972 edition, with a foreword and epilogue.

Wilson, Gary, Greg Wilcox, and Chet Richards (2005), "4GW and OODA Loop Implications of the Iraqi Insurgency," briefing at Australian War College, 12-14 April 2005. Online: www.au.af.mil/au/awc/awcgate/ssi/wilcox-panel-apr05.pdf [accessed 22 January 2009].

# About the Author

Daniel Ford is a New Hampshire-based writer, best known for his prize-winning history of the American Volunteer Group, the "Flying Tigers" of Burma and China in the early months of the Pacific War, 1941-1942. He was a reporter for *The Nation* in South Vietnam, an experience that gave him an abiding affection for the U.S. Army's Special Forces troops, along with grist for a novel that became the acclaimed Burt Lancaster film, *Go Tell the Spartans*. He has written other works of fiction with a military-historical twist, set in World War II and during the Irish rebellion and civil war early in the 20th Century.

In 2006, Ford enrolled in an online master's program at King's College London, studying War in the Modern World with an entering class of mid-career military officers and civilians from the United Kingdom, Sweden, Germany, Denmark, Singapore, and the United States. *A Vision So Noble* is based on the papers he wrote for that course of study, and especially on his concluding dissertation (which received the highest possible grade, the first time an A++ was ever awarded in the program).

A list of his books can be seen online at www.danfordbooks.com

Printed in Great Britain
by Amazon